Welcome to 'How To Become a Pilot' – The ultimate guide to getting your pilot licence and finding a fulfilling career. This is written to help others realise their dreams and is updated annually to ensure it's as relevant as possible.

ISBN – 13: 9798328475174

Firstly, I'd like to say a big personal thank you for your purchase!

This is the second book I've written and it's involved a lot more work than the first!

Whilst the first book 'How To Become An Airline Pilot' draws on my experience and research from within the airline industry specifically, this new book opens up to a much wider audience and required a substantial amount more of research.

As well as drawing from my own background and network within the broader aviation world, I've spent copious months filtering through the masses of information out there in search of the most up to-date & relevant material to make this book as valuable as possible to you. A lot of time and effort has gone into researching, writing, and putting it all together.

Your small investment in this book will hopefully pay off multiple times over in various ways during the journey you go on after reading it.

During the writing process, I reached out to some of the aviation companies I thought most relevant to the readers. Some of them very kindly offered discounts to readers of this book, so please don't forget to check out the 'Discounts & Recommendations' section at the end!

If you have any questions or feedback, please feel free to email team@pilotbible.com or get in touch via our social channels.

 A review would mean the world!

If you find the book helpful, words can't express how grateful I'd be if you could spend 30 seconds leaving an Amazon review by scanning the QR code so that this book can bring value to many others like you!

Scan To Review

www.PilotBible.com

Table of Contents

Introduction

What Is This Book?

This is a guide to provide you with an overview of how the modern-day aviation industry works, how you go about getting a pilot's licence and insights into the opportunities that await you once you've got one.

The aim is to simplify the overly complexed world that aviation has become. It's a sector that's constantly changing. Job opportunities and roles are always evolving, as are the rules, requirements and regulations governing them. I've focused on breaking down complicated topics and presenting them in comprehensible formats.

It's a compilation of 20+ years of my own research gathered through a mix of first-hand experiences along with interviews from colleagues and connections across the aviation industry (along with lots of time on the web ensuring it contains the most up-to date and accurate information possible).

Whether you're in school trying to decide which subjects to take or you're in mid-life & considering a career change, this book will give you a better understanding of what's available out there and what the different careers in aviation involve, giving you a clearer picture of how to take the first steps in the direction that's right for you.

It's the book I wish existed when I was making my own decisions about which aviation path was right for me.

Why Have I written It?

From a young age I knew I wanted to become a pilot but wasn't sure which path to take to get there. I wasn't entirely sure how many different flying jobs existed let alone what each one *really* entailed. Frustratingly, there was nothing out there to give me a clear understanding of all the options available to me.

The closest I came to such a thing was attending an aviation career fair. Whilst career fairs are a great way to see a few of the options out there, there's a big catch with them. You see, companies usually have to make an investment of time and money to exhibit at a career fair. Whilst we all like to believe these large companies truly have our best interests at heart, unfortunately there's often one major motive these companies have to be exhibiting and it's one that makes their investment worthwhile....money. Specifically, your money.

Most flight schools and aviation organizations that exhibit at these fairs exist because they make profit every time they get a student through their doors, so companies marketing themselves at career fairs can often be biased and will say what you want to hear to get you to sign over a few years of your life & often a substantial sum of money to them. You have to be careful and take their marketing pitch with a pinch of salt.

Another way I'd try to source my information was scouring the internet for hours each day. Unfortunately, the most helpful material was usually hard to find, often buried deep within forum threads. Even when I did eventually locate part of what I was looking for, it was usually very limited and more often than not extremely outdated.

I couldn't believe there wasn't a non-biased, up-to date guide out there capable of giving someone interested in an aviation career a clear understanding of what options are available to them, along with what life would be like should they choose to embark on that journey.

To my great surprise 2 decades later, there still doesn't seem to be anything out there that compiles exactly the above. Whilst a few books out there provide information on very specific paths (such as the journey to being an airline pilot) there aren't any that cover the vast array of different options out there. Given my background and time spent within the global aviation community, I thought it give it a crack at being the person to create it!

Aviation is still a relatively secretive world. It's incredibly hard for those on the outside (& even on the inside!) to get a really clear understanding of the day-to-day life of specific pilot roles unless you happen to know one. Even then, they aren't usually job roles that you can shadow someone in or do work experience with to get a feel for it. Due to the above it's hard to know what a certain pilot job truly entails until you've committed a lot of your time and money to start doing that job yourself.

I want to do my best to lift this veil of secrecy and arm you with all the facts enabling you to make the most informed decision possible about your future. I also want to manage your expectations in order to increase your level of satisfaction when you move into a future role that is a good fit for you.

Why Me?

Whilst becoming a commercial airline captain at age 28 was a huge personal achievement for me, that alone doesn't give me much credibility to put this book together.

What I believe does however, are my endeavours on the side of my airline career & the way I've immersed myself within various parts of the aviation industry over the last 2 decades.

Whilst for most people an airline pilot job may be enough, I wanted to continue exploring different aviation sectors & had a hunger to constantly learn more about the industry. I wanted to know about each and every opportunity out there for pilots, so much so that I took the decision to go part time with the airlines to give me more time to do just that, whilst simultaneously setting up a website to help with my quest.

Pilotbible.com has actually turned out to be the foundation for this book. It's a site designed to give people insights into 'A Day In The Life' of different pilot jobs around the world. I've since interviewed dozens of extremely interesting and impressive pilots who have been kind enough to share their story on the site.

Through a mix of opportunities created by the website along with my own desire to explore the industry further, I've ended up doing some incredible things and meeting lots of incredible people, whilst also gaining real insights and understanding into parts of the industry most people may not get to see.

My own flight training journey took me from flying helicopters in the US to flying Cessna's across New Zealand before I was in my 20's. I've since held an array of aviation-based positions from refuelling Spitfires for a flight experience company to writing a monthly column for a well-known aviation magazine in the UK.

I've personally been through the extremely rigorous UK military pilot selection process, and over the last decade have been lucky enough to spend time staying on various military bases including RAF Lossiemouth (a fast-jet base) and RAF Odiham (Chinook helicopter base).

Whilst working for an aviation tech startup in London I spent much of my time traveling around the UK meeting with flying schools and operators. That role took me as far afield as Texas where we exhibited at the infamous Heli-Expo, which in turn led to some unreal opportunities such as low level flying through the Californian canyons and flying through central London in an A109.

More recently I wanted to explore the charitable side of aviation and have joined an aid organization that not only runs flying experience days for children in the UK, but also organizes international aviation aid for disaster struck countries, giving me a real insight into this side of things.

As well as giving me invaluable firsthand experiences, all these roles and adventures have given me a wide range of contacts spanning various parts of the industry, and I've been able to draw on their knowledge and experience to piece this book together. Although I've still had to do lots of research & fact checking to ensure the book's as accurate as possible, hopefully you'll feel that I'm in a reasonably good position to condense much of the complexity of the aviation world into a book.

I still operate as an airline captain and monthly columnist, whilst also releasing regular content and conducting interviews on Pilotbible.com to continue to bring as much value to others as I can.

How To Use It

I've split the book into 2 main sections. The first breaks down licensing, requirements and all the admin side of flying, whilst also explaining how you go about obtaining the type of pilot licence that's right for you. The second section is essentially a career options guide giving you an idea of all the different types of pilot jobs and careers available out there, put together from a mix of interviews with colleagues, friends and other connections operating in those jobs, as well as my firsthand research going out to experience the roles (please note there are almost certainly other niche jobs out there not mentioned in the book, but I've done my best to cover all I can!).

Each job role comes with a description of what the job itself actually entails, along with what the day to day is really like. I've also listed the requirements needed to get those jobs. Having a good understanding of the various roles and their requirements will give you a clearer picture of which training path is right for you.

Questions for you

Before we dive into the core of the book, there are two important questions you should take some time ask yourself:

Do you want to fly for fun or as a job?

It's important to stress how different these two are.

Flying for fun is just that.....fun! It will be a hobby. Flying for fun gives you ultimate freedom; you choose when and where you fly, along with who you fly with. If at any point you stop finding it fun, you can simply stop doing it.

Flying for a job on the other hand entails being told where you're flying, the days/hours you're going to be flying, and who you'll be flying with. A job in aviation is usually a lifestyle as well a job. It's not for everyone and it's essential you understand the difference.

Your answer to this question will dictate which type of licence you need along with the medical and experience requirements that go with it. It's also something you should be clear about early on, to minimize the chance of you ending up in a situation that you don't feel fulfilled in.

If you don't know your answer yet, hopefully a read of this book along with some reflection time will get you closer to it.

Why do you want to be a pilot?

Similar to the previously question but slightly different. I'd strongly recommend you find some time to really think about this one.

Ask yourself *why* you want to be a pilot. Be totally honest. What are the first things that come to mind? Is it the physical act of flying? The expected feeling of freedom? Is it the idea of being part of a team conducting challenging missions? Grab some paper and write out all the things that pop into your head.

Focus on whatever crops up and go a level deeper, asking *why* again.....*why* do you desire those things or feeling?

Once you've got to the next layer of your answers, consider if becoming a pilot is really the best way to achieve those desires, needs or wants? Aviation is a notoriously challenging and expensive industry to get into and stay in. Are there other ways to achieve those things you desire that may have an easier path to get there?

Sometimes there aren't, in which case a career in aviation is likely for you! But sometimes there are simpler ways and you don't necessarily need to enter a career in aviation to achieve them.

If 'money' or 'status' crop up, there's absolutely nothing wrong with that (they're both human nature!) just be aware that pursuing it for those things alone will likely lead to you feeling unhappy and unfulfilled in this career.

I'm asking you to do this now because whilst aviation can be an extremely rewarding career path, any aviator will tell you it will almost always be a very challenging one and require a lot of sacrifice.

I'm not trying to scare you here, but you deserve a reality check that flight schools probably won't give you. I have nothing to gain or lose so I'm here to tell you the truth.

There are varying pros and cons that come with different pilot jobs, and often a con for one person could be a pro for someone else. As such, I won't be labelling various parts as pros or cons in when we get into the job section, rather just detailing the elements.

What I *can* tell you is that most flying jobs will very likely involve the following in some capacity:

- High initial cost to get the required licence & flight experience
- Shift work & weekend work
- Often long, unpredictable and inflexible hours
- The nature of flying means you may be away from home a lot
- The sense of freedom and autonomy can often be less than what people expect when you're flying as a job
- Highly challenging & demanding situations
- Some flying jobs can be very weather dependant
- Aviation is notorious for being low paid in the first few years, but you can become highly paid as you progress
- Strain on yourself and the relationships around you due to all the above

I promise things will get more positive from here on out, but it's important you consider all of the above. There's no shame in changing your mind about things. My airline pilot training course had many people dropout throughout the process. If your heart isn't in it for the long haul, it's better to do the research and figure this out now instead of getting an unwanted surprise and regretting anything a few years down the line!

This is not a question of whether you can or you can't become a pilot. I'm positive that by the end of this book, if you want it, you can. It's a question of whether you *actually* want it, deep down, and whether this is the right industry for you to be getting into. Are the potential sacrifices worth the end goal for you? Do you want it enough? Only you know the answer to those.

Research

Whilst this book serves as an overview and guide to the different options available out there, it doesn't substitute for your own in-depth research.

If there's a career option you come across in the book that you like the sound of, the next most important thing to do is dive headfirst into your own research around that job.

Any time that you can put into research now could save you an unfathomable amount of time in the future in preventing you entering a career that turns out to be not quite right for you.

Your aim with the research is to get the best possible understanding of what the job actually entails, in order to figure out if it's something you could actually see yourself doing as a career.

Research Methods

To get the best idea of what a job really entails, you need to be trying to immerse yourself in that world. Whilst reading books and browsing videos/articles on the web can be a good start, you need to get out there and connect with the people currently doing the job. Ways I'd suggest are:

- Find pilots in your network that do the specific job you're interested in. If you have any family friends, or friends of friends that know of any current pilots, ask for their number and give them a phone call. Ask them to be candid about their lifestyle & job and not to sugarcoat it.
- LinkedIn – It may seem ballsy, but it's paid dividends for me in the past. If you don't have any pilots in your network doing the job you're interested in, LinkedIn is a great way to reach out to a few pilots that work for the company or in the sector you'd like to work for. You can easily search by company and directly message pilots who work there (register for a 'free trial' with Premium if you need to then cancel before the trial ends). My advice would be rather than bombarding someone with lots of questions in the first message, let them know your situation and ask if they could spare 5 minutes for a call to really

help you out. Try and contact a few different people and expect rejections or non-replies. Don't take them personally. Eventually you'll get someone who says yes.

- Base visits – Interested in working for a certain company, or already decided what type of pilot you want to be? Speak to that company directly. Ask if you can come and see their base & spend some time with their pilots. Again, expect rejections, but you also might be surprised at how willing and open some companies are to help you out.
- Online blogs – there are many blogs/vlogs out there detailing the day to day life. PilotBible's 'Day In The Life' section was built exactly for this purpose. Lots of pilots from different parts of the industry share insights into their day to day working lives. It's worth checking out. There are various other pilot blog/vlogs out there but be careful, some may be glamourized to get more views.
- Online forums – There are some superb online forums out there specifically for pilots & those looking to get into the aviation world. Proffesional Pilots Rumour Network – Pprune.org is one of the most popular and has everything from threads about specific airlines, to students sharing their experiences at certain flight schools.
- Career fairs – A great way to meet pilots whilst also seeing what opportunities the industry has to offer, but with the caveat mentioned about them in the previous section.
- Ask me! Always feel free to drop me an email at team@pilotbible.com and I'll endeavor to get back to you.

Whilst you may feel guilty taking up someone's time that you barely know, most pilots will be happy to help you out and give you time. We were all in a similar position at one point!

Requirements

There are certain requirements you will need to get started in the industry and these can be broken down into *education, medical, flight experience* and *age*. It's important to note that requirements are subject to change and are also different country to country.

Educational Requirements

You do not *need* a degree to become a pilot. This is a common misconception. Infact, you could technically become a pilot with 0 schooling education qualifications at all. If you have the money and the cognitive ability, there's nothing stopping you funding your own flight training privately and working your way up through the licences (providing you can pass all the written & practical examinations).

Employers and major flight training schools however will often stipulate their own education requirements in order to land a place with them.

As the education requirements vary sector to sector, company to company, and are also constantly changing, it's impossible to list them all here in detail so you'll have to do your research into the exact requirements for your chosen career path, but to give you an idea of what I'm talking about;

If you wanted to become an airline pilot and go through a large flight training school, basic requirements in the UK to apply to such a flight schools are currently 5-6 GCSE's, or equivalent, grade A-C (5-9). Airlines can then be more specific when recruiting pilots. British Airways for example states that 3 of those GCSE subjects must be Mathematics, English and Science.

In the US, similar flight schools require a high school GPA of 3.0 or two years of college experience. Major airlines in the US used to require a bachelor's degree, but with the current pilot shortage, this is no longer the case. Whilst a degree may help your application, know that it's currently not a necessity.

Please note the above is a requirement if you're joining big flight schools on integrated training schemes (explained in the next section). There is absolutely no education level requirement to walk into your local flying club and begin flying lessons.

To apply to join the Royal Air Force in the UK as a pilot, you currently need 5 x GCSE's grade C/4 or above, along with 2 A-Levels grade C or above. To apply to join the US military you do still need a minimum of a bachelor's degree.

If you don't have the required educational grades for the job role you'd like to go into, I'd absolutely recommend you contact the employer or flight school anyway to let them know where you're at with things (they may be able to help).

For those interested in gaining a degree and unsure of whether to do that first, we have an entire blog post on that at PilotBible.com. Some flight schools now offer courses where you study for a degree alongside your flight training which is a great way to kill two birds with one stone. More info in that post!

 ## Age Requirements

You can start having flying lessons at whatever age you want. Age restrictions vary country to country, but you can usually fly solo as young as 16 year old (solo means you're still 'training' and don't have a license, but you're flying alone in the aircraft under the supervision of an instructor who will be on the ground). 17 is the youngest age at which you can gain a pilot's license.

If you're wanting a career in the airlines and looking to join a large airline training school, you can usually apply at 17 but not begin flight training until your 18th birthday as this is the minimum age for the type of licence you'll be getting there ('Commercial Pilots Licence' or 'Frozen Airline Transport Pilots Licence'). You have to be 21 to gain a fully unrestricted 'Airline Transport Pilots Licence', although there are ways to fly an airliner without this. Don't worry, we'll go into what all these licences mean shortly.

The UK Air Force currently only take pilot applicants between 17.5 and 23 years old, whereas the US Air Force accept applications from 18 – 30. The UK Navy accept pilot applicants up to 25 years old and Army up to 30.

There is currently no *upper* age limit to hold a pilot's license however pilots *must* retire from commercial flying when they hit age 65 in both the UK and US. They can still operate private aircraft.

 Medical Requirements

This is an important one! You'll be required to hold some sort of medical certificate before you get anywhere near gaining a pilot's license. You go about this by visiting an Aviation Medical Examiner (AME) who will assess you.

There are 3 levels of aviation medication certificate:

Class 1

The highest level of medical certificate you can get in aviation, and therefore the most stringent.

It's a high cost to get your initial Class 1medical done (currently £700/$800). After this & throughout your career you'll be required to renew your medical certificate annually at a minimum. The cost for renewal each year sits at around £250/$300, but most airlines and large employers will re-imburse you for this renewal cost each year once you're employed.

It's a very thorough examination and can take up to 4 hours.

The examination will include the following:

- Medical history
- Eyesight
- Physical examination
- Electrocardiogram (ECG)
- Lung function test
- Haemoglobin blood test
- Urine test

Class 2 & 3

These are certificates that you'll need to visit an AME for, however the initial medical checks will be less stringent than a Class 1 and the certificate will be valid for longer. They're generally used for lower classes of licences as shown on the table on page 22.

Medical certificates only last for a set amount of time, after which they must be renewed. In the UK, Class 1's must be renewed every 12 months. This then drops to 6 months above a certain age. Class 2 & 3's are valid for 60 months, but again this limitation reduces as you get older. Check your licence issuing authority's website for the latest information on exact age restrictions for renewals. Any changes to your health must always be reported to your AME, who holds the power to revoke your medical certificate at any stage. Without a current medical certificate, you will not be allowed to fly.

If you're sure you want a career flying aircraft, I'd strongly recommend you invest in a medical **before** you go much further.

Getting this done early gives you lots of time to explore any potential issues you may face. It could bring up something that may temporarily prevent you from getting a certain class certificate until the problem is sorted out. Worst case, it may highlight something that will preclude you from ever gaining a certain class and therefore decide your career options for you. As disheartening as that could be, it's best to know this before investing too much time or money into things.

We'll go into the meaning of all the licenses in the next section, but to show you how the requirements for each certificate class vary slightly between countries;

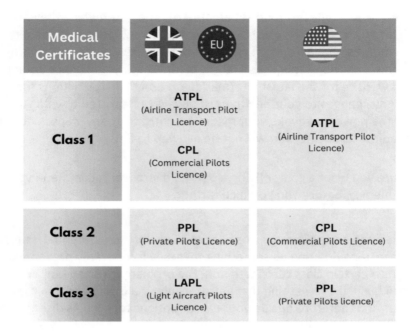

Medical Certificates	🇬🇧 🇪🇺	🇺🇸
Class 1	**ATPL** (Airline Transport Pilot Licence) **CPL** (Commercial Pilots Licence)	**ATPL** (Airline Transport Pilot Licence)
Class 2	**PPL** (Private Pilots Licence)	**CPL** (Commercial Pilots Licence)
Class 3	**LAPL** (Light Aircraft Pilots Licence)	**PPL** (Private Pilots licence)

To book yourself a Class 1, 2 or 3, simply visit your aviation authority's website (CAA in the UK, FAA in the US or EASA in Europe) and they should have links to certified AME's in their medical section.

 Flight Experience Requirements

Pilot licenses are partially based on hours of flight time you've amassed. This means to you need to build flight time and then sit certain exams once you've met the threshold for the minimum amount of flight hours required for that license type. This can vary from a minimum of 30 hours (Light Aircraft Pilots License) through to a minimum of 1500 flight hours (Airline Transport Pilots License) before being granted that license. Pilots used to keep all their hours logged in paper logbooks but nowadays most use digital ones. I've placed recommendations at the end of the book for the best digital logbooks to use. I've also created tables at the start of the next few sections detailing how many flight hours are required for each licence.

Licencing

Licence Issuing Authorities

Before we crack on to the juicy part, getting to grips with this slightly less exciting sounding section will give you a really good foundation when it comes to understanding how pilot licencing works.

Each nation has its own licence issuing authority, usually run by the government. In the US, it's the **Federal Aviation Authority (FAA).** In the UK, it's the **Civil Aviation Authority (CAA)** and in Europe it's the **EU Aviation Safety Agency (EASA).**

Whilst some nations allow you to operate from within their nation using a licence from another authority, not all do so it's important you gain the right licence for the geographical area you wish to land a flying job in.

i.e If you're looking to be based in the EU, you'll want to apply for an EASA licence. If looking in the UK alone, you'll apply for a CAA licence. You can be 'dual rated' which means you could end up with both a CAA and EASA licence, although you'll have to sit some quite a few exams twice over.

Being dual rated opens up your job opportunities and could make you more employable. It's not the end of the world if you're not dual rated. Most pilots I know aren't. As long as you have your end role in sight and know under which authority the licence must be held. There are usually conversion courses available further down the line if you did wish to convert your licence across.

Licence Types

There are a fair few different types of pilot licence available out there. It can all get pretty complicated quite quickly so I've done my best to simplify things into diagrams and lay this section out as clearly as I can.

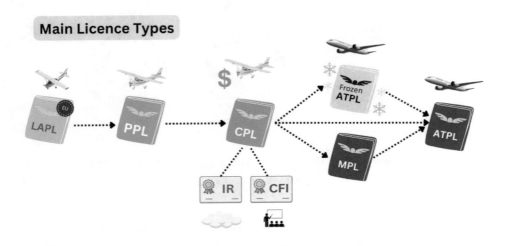

Main Licence Types

Light Aircraft Pilots Licence (LAPL)

LAPL was introduced in 2012 across Europe to enable a more accessible entry point into aviation for those interested in recreational flying. It allows you to act as pilot in command of a light aircraft with fewer hours of training and less stringent medical requirements compared to the PPL, although overall it's a more restrictive licence. You're more restricted on the type and weight of aircraft you can fly, along with where you can fly (you can only fly within Europe). With an LAPL, you also can't add an instrument rating onto your licence (explained shortly).

Although it only requires a minimum of 30 hours before you can take your test, you have to then complete another 10 hours of solo flying before being allowed to take any passengers.

The LAPL is a cheaper initial step to gaining an aviation licence, however most people tend to skip this and go straight for the PPL as it can be more cost effective in the long run.

If the initial cost of a PPL is just out of reach but an LAPL within, you are able to convert an LAPL to a PPL in the future with a few hours of extra training and written tests. I'd recommend really doing your further research if an LAPL is something you'd consider. Utilize forums such as PPrune.com.

Private Pilots Licence (PPL)

This is the baseline licence for most pilots. A PPL allows you to act as the pilot in command of an aircraft privately, without renumeration. There are often restrictions on the aircraft weight and number of passengers you can take even with the licence (in the UK it's a 5750kg aircraft and 19 passengers). It's typically used for personal travel, recreation or non-commercial purposes.

You cannot be paid to fly with a PPL, meaning essentially you cannot get a flying job that re-imburses you for your flying services. You can however cost share if you're taking other passengers, whereby everyone pays a % of the flight cost, but you must also contribute an equal share of the money.

A PPL is traditionally the first rung of the ladder for anyone wanting a career in aviation. It requires around 40 hours of flight time along with passing multiple written exams & a practical test. It also only requires one of the lower class medical certificates.

Commercial Pilots Licence (CPL)

For anyone looking to actually get paid to fly, a CPL is imperative. It's the natural next step from a PPL and gaining a CPL enables you to work for commercial operations in return for renumeration.

To gain a CPL you need to complete a substantial number of flying hours after you've passed your PPL (usually 150-200 hours in total) along with more comprehensive written exams and a practical test. You'll often also need a higher class of medical certificate.

Airline Transport Pilots Licence (ATP/ATPL)

Most people can have a very fulfilling career in aviation with just a CPL (and a few additional 'ratings' which we'll get onto shortly), however for those with their sights set on flying very large aircraft or the airlines, often a further type of licence will be required; an Airline Transport Pilots Licence.

An ATPL/ATP allows you to act as pilot in command of an aircraft for airlines and other large operators. It's the highest level of pilot licence certification. It requires a minimum of 1500 flight hours, along with extensive written exams and practical tests. It will also require a Class 1 medical certificate.

There is one caveat that allows you to fly an aircraft usually requiring an ATPL, but when you don't quite have the flight time; it's called a 'Frozen ATPL'.

Frozen ATPL/ATP

If you gain your CPL, along with an Instrument Rating (explained shortly), *and* you sit and pass the 13 ATPL written theory exams with a pass mark of 75% of more, you can combine these into a **'Frozen ATPL'**. This license allows you to apply for jobs and operate as a first officer or co-pilot. In these jobs you will always be operating with a captain who holds a full ATPL.

To turn a frozen ATPL it into a full ATPL (a process thoughtfully termed 'unfreezing'), you'll have hit 1500 flying hours and then sit a practical ATPL skills test (usually some manual flying exercises in the simulator). This unfreezing process has to happen within a time limit (currently 7 years from gaining your Frozen ATPL). You then have a fully unrestricted ATPL!

Multi-Crew Pilots Licence (MPL)

MPL is a relatively new licence in the industry, and it achieves the same end goal as a frozen ATPL; getting you a fully unrestricted ATPL, but in a slightly different way to the frozen ATPL path. It's now widely recognized and hugely popular amongst training schools and airlines alike. It's only applicable to fixed wing aircraft at the moment.

With an MPL course, you don't go through the process of gaining your PPL, CPL, etc. Instead, you hit a set number of required flight hours in specific training aircraft types, before moving on to the next phase of training, not necessarily getting any licences along the way. A very large portion of your training will actually be spent in large simulators rather than flying real aircraft.

The MPL is a more modern way of training airline pilots. It's technically more restrictive than a frozen ATPL as it only allows you to operate in the exact multi-crew environment you've been trained for, however it will often get you to the front seat of a jet much faster. You'll be arguably more comfortable than your ATPL counterparts operating the jet when you start flying with your airline since the training is focused on your end aircraft type from the start.

You'll spend much longer in the simulator of the large jet aircraft you'll eventually be flying (up to 200 hours) and spend much less time in a smaller aircraft (often around 85 hours). You'll also be using your company specific operating procedures throughout the entirety of those 200 simulator hours which means you'll be much better prepared when you start operating for real.

The above means an MPL course is often shorter and cheaper than gaining a Frozen ATPL.

Once you hit 1500 hours, you can convert your MPL into an ATPL through sitting the same skills test as if you had a Frozen ATPL.

I joined the airlines through one of the first ever MPL courses and believe it's one of the main reasons I was able to get my command at a young age. Whilst larger aviation operators were initially apprehensive when this new license was introduced, they're mostly now in agreement that it's a much more efficient and effective way to train candidates who want to end up in the airlines. Most airlines will now have their own MPL schemes run by large flight schools.

In the USA/Canada, the government stipulate what's known as a '1500 hour rule' meaning you need 1500 flight hours before you can take the step into a jet. Due to this the MPL hasn't really taken off (pun intended), although some schools do offer it. Those MPL courses will involve lots of time in the simulator, but you'll also gain a CFI rating and therefore be able to teach other student how to fly whilst building towards your 1500 hours.

Fixed Wing vs Rotary Licences

Aviation is fundamentally divided into two main categories of aircraft: Fixed-wing and rotary. Fixed-wing aircraft (we know them as aeroplanes) have wings that remain stationary and generate lift through the aircrafts forward motion, typically powered by jet engines or propellers. They are suited for longer distances, higher speeds, and efficient cruising at high altitudes.

Rotary aircraft such as helicopters generate lift through rotating blades or rotors that spin around a mast. This allows them to take off and land vertically, hover, and perform agile manoeuvres in confined spaces, making them ideal for short distances, low-altitude flights, and operations requiring flexibility and precision.

It's important to note that although the overall licencing structure (PPL, CPL, ATPL etc) is similar when it comes to comparing rotary and fixed wing, they are very much separate entities from each other. Gaining a licence for one category of aircraft doesn't allow you to fly aircraft from the other.

To help clarify the difference, licences often have A for Aeroplane or H for Helicopter after them, i.e PPL (A) or PPL (H). Whilst there is some crossover with written exams, and you can count flying hours from one category of aircraft towards another licence in some instances, they are very different worlds and require very different training and licencing. This is why I've divided the jobs section later on into fixed wing and rotary.

Other Pilot Licences

Aswell as the above types of licences, there are a few more niche licences that are specific to certain aviation activities that I feel are worth a mention:

Sailplane Pilot Licence (SPL)

An SPL allows you to act as pilot in command of a sailplane, otherwise known as a glider. The course for this can be as little as 15 flying hours, along with written theory examinations and a practical skills test. In the UK it also requires you to have completed 45 launches and landings along with a cross country flight (not actually across country borders, it just means flying a certain distance).

To carry passengers, you'll need to complete a further 10 hours of flight time or 30 launches after you've gained your licence. To receive any kind of commercial payment for flying the glider you'll need to ammas 75 hours of flight time or 200 launches along with a further proficiency check.

Balloon Pilots Licence (BPL)

This will allow you to act as pilot in command on balloons and airships. Similar to the SPL, you don't need any other type of flying licence before doing this, although you will of course need a medical certificate.

The licencing requirements for balloons are quite varied depending on your country so I'd advise you to look at your licencing issuing authorities website for more detailed information, but to give you a brief overview;

Balloons tend to be split into different classes based on the balloons size. You'll take your training course on one class and then be qualified to fly that class only. A course usually consists of around 15 hours of flying, with around 20 landings/takeoffs and 10 inflations.

You'll then need to build your flight time on that class of balloon before being able to take a test to fly a larger class of balloon.

Ratings

This is a term you've likely heard thrown around if you've already explored aviation a little. A rating is essentially an optional addition to your licence. It's not a new licence in itself but allows you to do more with the licence you have.

Instrument Rating (IR)

When you first gain a PPL or CPL, you will be only be allowed to fly in Visual Metrological Conditions (VMC) using Visual Flight Rules (VFR). This means you'll need to be able to see the ground at all times, and stay set distances away from any clouds or weather that will reduce your visibility out the window.

Given the unpredictability of the weather and how rare a clear sky day is in places such as the UK, only being able to fly when the visibility is good and always within visual contact of the ground can really limit the scope of your flying.

Technologies now exist both in the aircraft and on the ground that means pilots can fly aircraft with no visibility out the window and still be able to navigate safely, whilst always knowing exactly where they are. To be able to legally use these technologies and fly in what's known as Instrument Meteorological Conditions (IMC) using Instrument Flight Rules (IFR) you'll need to get an Instrument Rating (IR) added onto your licence.

To gain an IR you'll usually do a mix of classroom and practical based training, as well as written theory exams. You'll also have a practical skills test whereby you'll be expected to navigate the aircraft whilst wearing a 'hood' which will prohibit you from seeing out the window, to ensure you're navigating solely using instruments. Some of the course can usually be completed in a simulator too. There are a few different levels of IR but a full IR will require around 50 hours of flight time.

You never *need* to get an IR, but gaining one definitely makes you a much safer and more aware pilot as well as massively increasing your employability. It's essential if you're ever going to be flying in poor weather conditions, so many commercial operations will require you to have one.

Night Rating

Flying at night can be very different to flying in the daytime. Much greater risks come with it and therefore to be allowed to fly between the hours of sunset and sunrise, you'll need a night rating. This usually involves a few hours of night flying with an instructor followed by one or two on your own, which can often be done at the same time as gaining your PPL.

Certified Flight Instructors Rating (CFI/FI)

Gaining a flight instructor rating enables you to provide flight instruction to student pilots, both classroom based and in the aircraft. Whilst it can be an extremely rewarding career in itself, most pilots use this rating as a stepping stone to build hours towards their next licence.

You'll usually need to hold a minimum of a CPL before you can apply to gain an FI. Pilots working towards an ATPL will often gain an FI rating as soon as they pass their CPL which allows them to build towards their 1500 flight hours whilst getting paid.

To gain an FI rating, you'll need to complete a flight instructor training course along with written knowledge tests focussed on instructional techniques. You'll also need to pass a practical flight test.

Aerobatics Rating

In order to legally perform aerobatics, you'll require an aerobatic rating. This advanced rating requires mastering complex manoeuvres such as loops, rolls, and spins under the guidance of an experienced instructor. It not only broadens a pilot's skill set but also deepens their understanding of aircraft dynamics and safety. It's also great fun!

What are 'Type Ratings'?

Aswell as having a pilot's licence, you'll need a type rating to be able to legally fly an aircraft. A type rating is essentially a clearance to fly a certain 'type' of aircraft. Someone who does all their fight training in a small propellor aircraft isn't allowed to just go and fly a jet the day they get their licence. A type rating course can be anything from a few hours with an instructor, to a month long course consisting of ground school, simulators and flying examinations in real aircraft.

In the UK you can get a Singe Engine Piston (SEP) rating which clears you to fly most single engine piston powered aircraft (small propellor aircraft). You'll usually automatically gain this rating if it's the type of aircraft you did your training & test in. You can then do a Multi-Engine Piston (MEP) rating course which will enable you to fly most twin engine propellor aircraft.

As the aircraft get larger than this however, the ratings become more specific (& more expensive!). If you wish to fly a Boeing 737, you'll have to do a specific type rating course for that aircraft alone (circa £30,000/$38,000). Having this rating only clears you to fly the Boeing 737. If you then wish to fly another large aircraft such as the Airbus A320, although it's an aircraft of similar size, you'll need to do a full A320 type rating course at a similar cost.

Some organisations will only accept pilots who are already type rated on the aircraft they're applying to fly. Others however will accept applications from those who don't have the type rating required for the aircraft that company operates. These are advertised as 'non type rated' roles. Usually, the company will either pay for your type rating outright when you join them, or they'll cover the cost of it but you'll pay it back to them over a set number of years. This is known as a *bond*.

Type Rating Instructor (TRI) & Type Rating Examiner (TRE)

TRI's and TRE's are essentially flight instructors and examiners who train and examine pilots that are gaining aircraft type ratings.

TRI's can conduct the training part i.e running the type rating ground school, flying and simulator training sessions. To gain a TRI rating you'll have to complete a TRI course along with passing an assessment of instructional skills and knowledge by a qualified examiner.

TRE's can do all of the above, and *also* conduct type rating skills tests, proficiency checks and examinations on pilots both in the simulator and in the aircraft.

A further training course along with written & practical exams is required to gain a TRE rating.

  Licencing Summary

- **PPL** is for non-commercial, recreational flying.
- **CPL** enables you to get paid to fly, but requires more advanced training and stricter medical requirements.
- **Frozen ATPL** is an IR, CPL and all ATPL written exams passed and allows you to act as a first officer or co-pilot of large aircraft.
- **ATPL** is the highest level of pilots licence and it's necessary for pilots operating on command of airliners or for very large complexed aircraft, requiring extensive experience and rigorous testing.
- **MPL** is a new type of licence that gets you to an ATPL in a more effective way than the traditional route of gaining your PPL then CPL.
- IR is an additional rating that allows for flying in poor visibility using instruments.
- CFI/FI rating allows pilots to teach and train new pilots.

- Type Ratings are required by all pilots to fly any sort of aircraft
- TRI/TRE can instruct and examine pilots as they gain type ratings for various aircraft

Pilot licences never expire, however ratings do. Ratings have to be renewed at intervals governed by your licence issuing authority.

For example in the UK, an IR is only valid for 25 months. An FI rating is valid for 36 months.

In terms of aircraft type ratings, the pattern tends to be the larger the aircraft, the more limiting the expiry time on the rating is. A rating to fly single engine pistons is valid for 2 years from the date of your test in the UK, whilst ratings for large commercial airliners are often only valid for one year.

When a rating is about to expire, they can be renewed by taking a practical skills test either in the aircraft or in a simulator. This isn't anywhere near the cost or time of the initial rating.

If you leave a rating expired for too long, there are different rules in place for how much training is required in order to revalidate that rating depending on how long it's been expired for.

Right, all of that out the way, let's move on!

Getting your licence

Every pilot's licence (& most ratings) will involve completing these 3 things;

- Written theoretical exams
- Minimum number of specific flight hours
- Practical skills test

Written Theoretical Exams

A large part of your flight training will actually be classroom based. You'll have to pass a variety of written exams and usually have to complete a set amount of ground based instruction preceding the test.

In the UK, to gain a PPL you'll have to be capable of passing the following 9 exams:

- Air law
- Human performance
- Meteorology
- Communications
- Principles of flight
- Operational procedures
- Flight performance and planning
- Aircraft general knowledge
- Navigation

If you then wish to apply for a CPL, you'll need to complete at least 350 hours of theoretical knowledge training, along with further written examinations. An ATPL will require you to sit 14 written exams!

The amount of time you are required to spend in a classroom will vary between licence and country, as well the exact exam topics you'll need to sit. It's best to speak to your local flying school or check your countries aviation licencing authority's website.

Minimum Number of Flight Hours

To obtain a pilot license, you'll also need to meet a minimum number of flight hours across a specific range of flying. Some of this will be 'dual instruction' which means flying with an instructor in the cockpit alongside you. Some of it will be 'solo' or 'pilot in command (PIC)' time, whereby you are the sole occupant of the aircraft. You'll likely also have to meet a requirement for cross country navigation flight hours. These are flight from one airport to another, and there's usually a minimum distance requirement between the two airfield for it to quality as cross country time.

As an example, for a UK PPL(A) the flight hour requirements are:

45 hours of flight instruction on aeroplanes, 5 hours of which may have been completed in an approved flight simulator training device, including at least:

- *25 hours of dual flight instruction,*
- *10 hours of supervised solo flight time, including at least 5 hours of solo cross-country flight time with at least 1 cross country flight of at least 270 km (150 NM) that includes full stop landings at 2 aerodromes different from the departure aerodrome.*

Again, the hour requirements for each licence and each country are different and constantly evolving. In an effort to keep this book as simple as possible, I've simplified the hours shown in the tables and I'll encourage you to do your own research to find out the exact hour requirements that apply to your country and licence type.

 # Practical Skills Test

Once you've passed all the written exams and gained the required flying hours, the final step is to pass a practical skills test. This will consist of a flight (or multiple) with an examiner next to you. They'll be assessing your proficiency in the aircraft and asking you to complete various handling manoeuvres and emergency drills. You'll be examined on everything you do and given a pass or fail at the end of the flight.

Flight Schools

As you can see, to get any sort of pilot's licence there's a lot involved. This is why it's important to have your end goal in mind as this will dictate the best way of going about undertaking your training.

If you're looking to fly just for fun i.e a PPL, then going down to your local flying school and completing the flying hours & exams with them will be a good option. The prices of lessons will vary slightly from school to school, but they're usually all quite competitively priced and it's often handy to train at a flight school very local to you as opposed to one much further away because it's a tiny bit cheaper. Being close to the field makes life easier with last minute weather disruption etc and also you'll be around to take any cancellations or slots that become available at short notice.

If however, you know you want to end up with a CPL with various add-ons, or an ATPL, there are other more efficient training options available to you.

The more traditional way (& still a perfectly ok way to do it) is to gain a PPL, then continue hour building for a CPL, and then hour build towards your ATPL. Usually, people would get a Flight Instructor (FI) rating after their CPL so they can essentially get paid to instruct people whilst building their own hours at the same time.

Whilst this more traditional method gives you a great variety of experience, it's a very long-winded way in comparison to what else is available out there now. That method also relies on you being able to land different jobs at various stages of your flying career on your path to getting your ATPL.

Nowadays, there are large flight schools whose sole purpose is to get someone with little to no flight experience into the front seat of an airliner or large commercial aviation operation in under 2 years.

Integrated vs Modular

There are two options when selecting a course with a big school. 'Integrated' courses will be full time, Monday – Friday and you'll likely be living on a campus, or very near the training school with other cadets. There's no need to get flying jobs during training, everything is covered by your initial training fee and you'll finish the course ready to step into the front seat of an a large passenger aircraft. These are intensive courses and you'll likely finish within 18 months – 2 years.

The other way is to take these courses as 'Modular', which means breaking the course down into stages, like the traditional way, and completing each as and when you wish to. Whilst it's a great option for someone who can't commit to the intensive course, it will end up taking longer to complete.

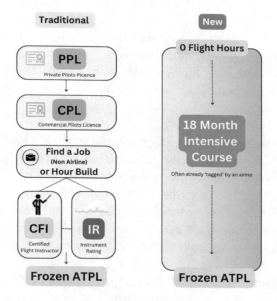

An example of some of these large schools for your reference;

- CAE – Based in the UK and US, they train airline pilots on both integrated and modular courses.
- ATP Flight School – They train US pilots on integrated courses to become airline pilots
- HeliCentre – Based in the UK, they train helicopter pilots from 0 hours right up until ATPL level on integrated and modular courses.

Military

Another route that should be taken into consideration is the military. Not only will you forge great bonds and enjoy epic adventures on this path, but the camaraderie you'll find there will be incomparable to much else. Another impressive perk.....You don't have to fork out a penny for flight training. The military will pay *you* to learn to fly!

To apply to the military as a pilot, you'll need to meet the entry requirements as dictated on their website or in their local career's office. You'll have to pass an extremely stringent selection process which will consist of aptitude tests, mathematics tests, group exercises, interviews, medical checks and potentially presentations to an audience. It's one of the hardest selection processes to get through but if it's something you really want and you prepare effectively, you'll stand a good shot at it.

If you're offered a place, you'll complete a 'basic training' phase before you get anywhere near the controls of an aircraft. This will often be a few month's worth of extremely hard work. This part is nothing to do with flying. You'll be training with all new joiners regardless of the military role they're going into. It's during this extremely testing training period that you'll be turned from a civilian into military personnel. It's also where the military try and weed out those who don't have what it takes, so expect to be pushed to your limits!

Once you've completed basic training phase, you'll then begin your flight training. Everyone will start flight training on small fixed-wing aircraft before being 'streamed' onto the aircraft type that they're eventually going to be flying. The military usually group their aircraft into fast jets (fighter jets), rotary (helicopters) and multi engines (larger fixed-wing transport aircraft) categories. Whilst you can select a preference, you often don't actually get to choose which type of aircraft you end up flying and you'll be streamed onto whichever aircraft the military need you to operate. It will often reflect how you performed during your flight training, with those streamed onto fast jets usually the top performing students during training.

This is definitely something you should take in consideration if your heart is absolutely set on flying a certain type of aircraft. If you want to fly a fast jet, the military is the only place you can do this so you'll have to join either way but it's worth being aware that you may not end up being streamed onto the category of your choice.

Please note some forces only operate certain categories of aircraft i.e the Army in the UK only operate helicopters, the Navy operate helicopters and fast jets, whereas the Royal Air Force (RAF) operate all 3 categories. It's worth checking this before deciding which force to apply to as once you're in a force you can only be streamed onto the aircraft they operate.

There are a few other things to consider with this route. There will be a 'minimum term of service' you'll have to complete; this usually sits somewhere between 8-12 years for a short commission. This minimum term is essentially so the military don't invest all this money into you, then you leave straight away (it costs the RAF an estimated £5million to train a fast Jet pilot. Fair enough!).

When you do leave the military after your service, you likely won't have the correct type ratings for other commercial aircraft. However, ex-military pilots are highly sought after in the aviation industry and lots of civilian companies offer specific military conversion courses.

With the military, you'll also be away from home a lot. You could be sent into hostile environments and war zones which brings with it obvious risks.

Another thing to consider nowadays is pilot training delays. In the UK at least, right now people are joining the RAF as 'Pilots' but due to a training backlog, having to wait up to 5 years until they can actually start pilot training. During this time, you'll likely be given office-based roles. Whilst this backlog is in the process of being cleared as I write, it is still there. It's worth asking your local military careers office about it, along with trying to find cadet pilots already in the pipeline for the most up to date news.

If it's a path you'd consider, my advice would be to go on base visits. Speak to your local military recruitment office and explain that you'd love to go and speak to pilots on the base of your choice. I did this when I was considering it, and it was unbelievably insightful. I stayed on a fast jet base followed by a helicopter base. It gave me a feel for everything and the opportunity to ask all the questions I wanted.

If you're still in school, college, or university, and interested in the idea of the military, I'd urge you to join the Air Cadets or University Air Squadron. You'll get a real feel for military life without having to fully commit, and you'll also get some free flying experience!

I'm yet to meet an ex-military pilot who didn't thoroughly enjoy their time there!

 ## Financing Training

If you don't go down the military route, it's likely that you'll have to privately fund your training (although there are exceptions that we'll talk about). The cost of your training will massively depend on what sort of licence you want to gain. Whilst a fixed wing PPL may only set you back £10,000/$14,000, anything above that will start to need some serious financial planning on your part.

The cost of a fully integrated ATPL/MPL course that will get you a job in the airlines currently sits at around £100,000/$120,000. This package includes everything; accommodation, training, exam fees etc. Modular is often cheaper as you're not paying for accommodation & various other bits. Now, you have a few different options here, and what the large flights schools and employers can offer to help you out financially is constantly evolving.

Most people don't have that sort of money sat around, so there are special banks out there who will loan you this money specifically for flight training (Optimum Credit in the UK). You can of course also look to borrow the money from a normal bank. Both types will often need the loan backed against a house or something of similar value.

Whilst paying for this type of integrated course is a very effective and efficient option, you obviously don't need to spend all this money. You can still go the more traditional route, getting your PPL then work your way up to a CPL. You can then get paid to fly and build your hours towards an ATPL.

It's worth bearing in mind however that although this may look cheaper initially, if your end goal is a job with the airlines then it's going to cost you a lot more in terms of time to build your flying hours using this traditional method. It will likely take you years, by which point you may have been better off financially by paying more upfront for a fast-track integrated course and landing a job with an airline much sooner, therefore earning a bigger salary quicker and paying off much of the training debt.

Word of warning: Be <u>extremely cautious</u> giving smaller flight schools large sums of cash up front. There has been a recent spate of smaller flight schools going bust and students loosing tens of thousands of pounds they'd paid into an upfront account. Ensure any money you do pay is protected. Large flight schools will often be very transparent about how your money is protected once handed over, smaller flight schools should be doing exactly the same!

Sponsored Courses

Some large flight schools have airlines or commercial operators that will 'sponsor' you on certain courses. Be aware, **there is a big difference between 'sponsor' and 'fully funded'.** 'Sponsor' still usually means you'll be expected to cover the cost of training, but they'll guarantee you a job at the end of the training course. Some large flight schools may actually finance a loan for you.

Part of the 'sponsor' offer will likely be that the flight school or final employer will 'pay back' the loan to you over a set number of years once you're fully employed and flying for them. This is known as a bond, or being *bonded* to the company you fly for. Be aware, often those on a bonded scheme will be on a smaller salary than those not, with the 'loan repayments' making up the difference. So whilst schools and employers may try to market these schemes as paying your loan money back for you, what they're actually doing is paying you a normal pilot salary and labelling part of that salary as your loan repayment.

If you choose to leave a company during your bond period, there will often be financial penalties involved. Each and every contract will be different, so be sure to read into the small print.

Hopefully the above gives you a general overview and an idea of what questions to ask each employer if looking at a sponsored scheme. Most major airlines in the UK and US now run sponsored schemes also offering employment at the end of your flight training, as do larger operators in the helicopter world such as Bristow.

Fully Funded Courses

Fully funded courses seem to only exist in the airline world currently. Back in the day (30-40 years ago) airline courses would all be 'fully funded'. If you passed selection day the airline would cover the cost of the entirety of your training.

Whilst this definitely hasn't been the case for the last few decades, fully funded courses are now making their way back into fashion. At the moment they're few and far between so they're incredibly competitive to get onto.

Current airlines offering fully funded courses in the UK are TUI and British Airways. EasyJet are expected to join them very soon. These are exactly as they sound; all training costs are covered by the airline. However, you *will* be on a reduced salary once you start flying for the airline for a set number of years. It's a great way of overcoming the large initial financial hurdle for many and opening the door to the industry for those who couldn't previously afford it.

I'm really happy they're making a re-appearance and it's the direction the industry is heading in. For more info on these schemes, search our site for the blog post on fully funded training.

If you do want to go down the airline route and get a place on one of these fully funded course, I'd strong suggest you to take a look at my first book 'How To Become An Airline Pilot'. If you can understand and apply the learnings from that book, it will give you a great shot at getting your place on a fully funded scheme should you wish to go down that route

Small Scale Sponsorship

There are also small-scale sponsorship schemes out there that can help you with gaining certain ratings or aspects of flight training. They're often provided by a small company or individuals and are definitely worth keeping an eye out for. Do some google searches to find them, and check places like Flight Training News, who each month include a list of live scholarships up for grabs. There are usually various schemes to help people gain PPL's & CPL's.

Fixed Wing Pilot Roles

Hopefully by now you have a good overview of what's required to gain a pilot's licence, but then what next? There are so many career options out there for pilots and I think it's important you're informed about what they are, and what they really consist of. We'll start with the fixed wing category.

The below table summarises the requirements for pilots looking to gain fixed wing licences in both the EU/UK and US.

Licensing Requirements Fixed - Wing	Privelidges	Hour Req	Written Exams	Medical Req	Estimated Total Cost
LAPL	Fly light aircraft up to certain weight	30 hrs flight training	9 x Written Exams	Class 3/LAPL	£7,000
PPL	Private flying with friends & family	45 hrs of flight training	9 x Written Exams	Class 2	£10,000
		40 hrs flight training	1 x Written Exam	Class 3	$14,000
CPL	Get paid for flying	150 hrs flight time	14 x Written Exams	Class 1	£45,000 (incl PPL cost)
		250 hrs flight time	1 x Written Exam	Class 2	$60,000 (inc PPL cost)
MPL	Operate large aircraft in multi-crew environment	240 hrs flight time	14 x Written Exams	Class 1	£100,000
ATPL	Act in Command of large passenger aircraft	1500 hrs flight time	14 x Written Exams	Class 1	£100,000
			1 x Written Exam		$110,000

To keep it simple I've added the basic overall hour requirements for each. If you want an even more detailed table that breaks down the exact type of flight training hours required for each licence (solo, cross country etc), check out our blog post on the PilotBible website. At the end of the day your flight school will also tell you the exact type of hours you require.

Now moving onto jobs. Whilst the following isn't an extensive list of every single possible job available in the fixed wing world, I believe I've managed to cover the vast majority of options available out there;

Sightseeing Pilot

Salary Range $-$$

Role: You'll be conducting aerial tours & providing passengers with scenic views from the aircraft. The role involves planning and executing safe and hopefully enjoyable flights, often over notable landmarks. You'll ensure all pre-flight preparations, including weather checks, aircraft inspections, and route planning, are meticulously completed.

This role requires excellent flying skills but also customer service abilities as you'll often be sharing a small aircraft with multiple passengers. You'll be a tour guide as well as a pilot. It's a job that can bring with it some really special experiences and you've usually got an aircraft full of very happy passengers. It can however get repetitive if you operate the same tour for a prolonged period of time. Many pilots use a role like this to get paid to build their flying hours before moving onto other roles.

We've got an awesome interview in our 'A Day In The Life' section with Karl, a sightseeing pilot from New Zealand who spends his days flying tourists around the stunning Milford Sound area.

Working Hours: Highly dependent on the operation, although due to the nature of sightseeing its usually daytime working hours and weather dependant flying. Often much of your flying will be done at weekend, however in popular tourist locations you'll likely be flying in the week too.

Requirements: Minimum of a CPL along with a type rating for the type of aircraft you'll be flying.

Flight Instructor

Salary Range $-$$

Role: You'll provide both ground and flight instruction for student pilots, covering fundamental aviation principles, flight manoeuvres, navigation, and emergency procedures. Flight instructors also prepare students for various licensing exams, including written and practical tests. This position demands excellent flying skills, a deep understanding of aviation regulations, effective teaching abilities, and the capacity to adapt to different learning styles. You'll also likely be operating experience flights and trial lessons.

This can be an extremely rewarding career as you forge bonds with your students and watch them progress. Unfortunately it's a notoriously low paid role as companies know that most instructors are doing it to hour build towards their next licence. It's also a role where you need to be fully focussed and have very high levels of situational awareness as you'll be handing controls of the aircraft to inexperienced students.

Working Hours: The hours can be quite sporadic and very weather dependant. You'll often only get paid for the hours you actually fly (or teach ground school), and smaller companies will only fly when a student books in.

Much of the work at smaller independent flight schools will often be centred around weekends as most flight students will tend to work during the week to fund their training. If you join a larger flight school offering integrated courses as an instructor, the work will generally be more consistent as the students are full time.

Requirements: CPL along with an FI rating (although some countries allow you to operate as an FI on just a PPL and a certain number of flying hours). In additional an IR rating will make you more employable as an instructor but it's not always necessary.

Bush Pilot

Salary Range $-$$

Role: You'll be operating aircraft in remote and rugged areas, often where conventional transportation is impractical. The role involves transporting passengers, cargo, and essential supplies to and from isolated locations, such as rural communities. Bush pilots must navigate challenging terrain, unpredictable weather, and unpaved airstrips, requiring exceptional flying skills and adaptability.

Usually, you'll be responsible for much more than just the flying and be wearing multiple other hats during the operation, from thorough pre-flight planning, including route selection and aircraft maintenance checks, to management and control of the cargo or passengers. These tend to be single pilot operations, so you'll often be operating alone with lots of different moving parts to manage.

A bush pilot requires sharp focus along with a high level of self-reliance and problem-solving abilities. It's a role that involves more threats than lots of other aviation roles, as such it's sometimes regarded as more dangerous.

Bush flying is a superb way to develop and hone your flying skills and most people tend to do it early on in their aviation careers to gain experience flying in varied & challenging environments whilst also getting paid to build hours.

Working Hours: Highly varied. Some companies will have contracts which require bush flying routes to be operated on a regular and consistent basis. Others may be more supply & demand based, leading to less predictable schedules. Often bush pilots will be living away from home whilst doing the job and it can be an all-encompassing lifestyle.

Requirements: Minimum of a CPL if you wish to get paid, along with a type rating on the aircraft you're wishing to fly. Some larger operations may require an ATPL if you're operating larger aircraft and loads.

Humanitarian Pilot

Salary Range $-$$

Role: This role is similar to a bush pilot in that you'll also be transporting cargo and passengers across a very diverse range of environments. Humanitarian pilots however often find themselves flying into disaster zones and conflict areas.

You'll usually be providing humanitarian aid and relief either after or during disasters around the world. The military sometimes provide this, however there are many non-governmental organizations (NGOs), international aid agencies and charitable organizations that serve the same purpose and require pilots to work for them. Examples of a few are AirServ and Aviation Sans Frontières.

Working Hours: Very varied. Usually supply and demand based work. When there is a disaster, you can expect to fly to the disaster zone and spend a lot of time away from home whilst on missions. Whilst this work isn't usually as dangerous as a bush pilot, it's very much still a lifestyle choice. You'll fly some amazing missions and work with the most incredible people, whilst also doing extremely meaningful work. The cost to you will be time away from home along with low pay and likely very long hours when on missions. You'll often be operating in 3rd world countries and likely without the same limitations and flight time protections you have when operating in countries such as the US or UK so the work can be very tiring.

Requirements: CPL minimum

Agricultural Pilot

Salary Range $-$$
Role: You'll be operating a crop dusting aircraft to apply fertilizers, pesticides,

herbicides, and seeds over agricultural fields. The role involves precise flying at very low altitudes to ensure even distribution of chemicals or seeds, constantly navigating obstacles such as power lines and trees. Whilst it's role that can get repetitive (flying up and down fields all day), you'll be operating at very low level and have to remain very fully engaged throughout.

Low hour CPL holders will usually do crop-dusting to build hours whilst also gaining the valuable experience of flying an aircraft at very low level with precision control.

Working Hours: Daytime hours, usually a stable and predictable working life.

Requirements: CPL

Survey Pilot

Salary Range $-$$

Role: You'll specialize in conducting aerial surveys and mapping missions using fixed-wing aircraft. The role involves flying over designated areas to gather data for various purposes such as land surveying, environmental assessments, infrastructure planning, and geological exploration.

Survey pilots use advanced equipment onboard to capture high-resolution images, collect geographic data, and create detailed maps and 3D models.

You'll collaborate closely with surveyors, engineers, and scientists to ensure accurate and comprehensive data collection. Some survey companies are government run and will employ military pilots, others are privately run and employ civilian pilots.

Working Hours: Daytime hours, usually a stable and predictable working life and often just Monday-Friday.

Requirements: CPL, relevant Type Rating and often an IR

Medical Pilot

Salary Range $-$$

Role: A fixed-wing medical/air ambulance/medevac pilot is responsible for transporting critically ill or injured patients between medical facilities quickly and safely. Their role involves operating specially equipped aircraft to provide rapid medical transportation, often from remote locations to areas with better equipped care.

You'll be part of the transportation link that's getting a patient to the best possible care. This could mean transferring patients from one hospital to another (via land ambulance transfers to/from the airports) which can sometimes mean travelling across international borders. If you're operating in sparse areas such as Australia, it could also mean flying directly to the scene of an accident and landing on the road. Although this is usually left to medical helicopter pilots, a pilot of a fixed-wing King Air medical aircraft did this in 2023!

You'll work closely with medical teams, ensuring the aircraft is prepared for patient care and equipped with necessary medical supplies.

Working Hours: Much of your roster is likely to be 'standby' time. Given the unpredictable nature of medical emergencies, it will be hard to know exactly what your flying schedule's going to look like very far ahead of time.

Every company will have different roster patterns but usually you'll operate for multiple days on standby, followed by multiple days off.

Requirements: CPL minimum almost certainly with an IR to enable you to fly even when the weather's not playing ball. Some operators will require you to have an ATPL.

Military Multi-Engine Pilot

Salary Range $-$$

Role: You'll be flying large multi-engine military aircraft such as the C-17 Globemaster or the C-130 Hercules. Your missions can be wide and varied, from transporting personnel and cargo to low level night flying through combat zones.

After you've been streamed onto 'multi-engines', you'll then be designated your exact aircraft type i.e C17 or C130. Depending on which aircraft type you become qualified on, you could be delivering humanitarian aid, providing surveillance overhead a conflict zone, or providing air to air refuelling for fighter jets.

Working Hours: Initial training tends to be mostly Mon-Fri hours, although you'll likely have to live either on base or extremely close to it during these training years. Once qualified you will travel away from home on 'tours' for multiple months at a time.

Requirements: Join the military, passing their selection process & basic officer training, followed by basic flight training before being streamed onto multi-engines.

Military Fast Jet Pilot

Salary Range $-$$

Role: This one's got to be the pinnacle of fixed wing flying for most people! As a fast jet pilot in the military, you'll operate state of the art fighter jets for air-to-air and air-to-ground combat missions.

The role includes conducting aerial patrols, engaging enemy aircraft, executing precision strikes, and supporting ground troops in conflict zones.

This position demands exceptional flying skills, strategic thinking, and the ability to perform effectively in high-pressure, dynamic combat environments.

High-speed low-level flying, landing on moving aircraft carriers and close formation flying are just a few of the very challenging tasks that fighter pilots will be carrying out in a day's work.

As a fast jet pilot, you'll need to maintain great physical fitness and mental acuity, as the g-forces induced from high speed manoeuvres can be extremely tough on the human body and the flying can be mentally fatiguing.

You'll be away from home a lot, but you'll also be doing one of the most wanted jobs out there with a tightly knit team of incredible people.

Whilst being a fighter jet pilot really is an incredible opportunity, you do need to remember that you are exactly that....a fighter pilot. There's a likelihood that at some point in your career you may have to take the life of another human being, purely because someone ordered you to. You may also find yourself fending for your own life. These aren't concepts to be taken lightly and you should consider how you feel towards them before applying.

Whilst the role often doesn't come with a huge level of pay, in the military lots of things are subsidized or free (accommodation, food, gym etc) so you're outgoings tend to be far less than in civilian life, enabling your pay check to go further.

Working Hours: Again the training years will tend to be mostly Mon-Fri hours. Once qualified, you'll be sent away on 'tours' for several months at a time. On some tours there will be routine flights conducted at the same time each day i.e patrols, whilst other flying missions will be more unpredictable. Missions whilst on tour will likely involve plenty of night flying.

Requirements: Join the military, passing their selection process & basic training, followed by basic flight training before being streamed onto fast jets. This is one of the longest training pipelines out there, taking between 6-9 years of rigorous training to master advanced flying techniques, weapon systems, and combat tactics before you're ready to fly a fast jet operationally.

Test Pilot

Salary Range $$-$$$

Role: This is an exciting role in which you'll be the first to fly new aircraft and test new developments of existing aircraft. You'll usually work directly for the aircraft manufacturers or be contracted out to them in order to put their aircraft through various test flights, operating to the edge of flight envelopes &

beyond. The aircraft will be loaded with various tracking sensors and equipment to help collect data to enhance development.

Working Hours: Usually a very stable and predictable working pattern if working for a large company such as Airbus. If working for a smaller company with experimental aircraft your hours could be more unpredictable.

Requirements: Test pilots are usually only taken from the military and often only those who have been trained on fast jets, or have gone through a military test pilot programme will be selected. Whilst you may be able to apply to civilian test pilot roles without military experience, you'll have to have a very impressive flying CV to get the job.

Coastguard Pilot

Salary Range $-$$$

Role: You'll be responsible for conducting aerial missions to locate and assist individuals in distress, often in remote or hazardous areas. The role involves flying aircraft equipped with specialized search and rescue equipment (most common aircraft are the C130 or King Air), performing systematic search patterns to locate missing persons, downed aircraft, or vessels in trouble. Coastguard pilots work closely with ground teams and rescue coordinators to relay information and guide rescue operations. You'll often have to navigate challenging weather conditions while prioritizing safety and mission effectiveness.

This position requires excellent flying skills, attention to detail, and the ability

to remain calm and decisive during time critical situations.
It also will require a lot of patience as you could find yourself conducting a search pattern over the sea looking for a missing person or vessel for multiple hours (so you'll also probably require a reasonably large bladder...)

Working Hours: You'll usually work multiple days at a time on standby, available to be called out anytime of the day or night. This will then be followed by a block of days off. Rosters are usually fixed and built in advance so you know when your days off will be.

Requirements: In some countries the Coastguard or Search & Rescue (SAR) is a government owned service, often run by the military & therefore the pilots are military pilots. This seems to be a changing theme however and more countries are privatising their SAR operations. The UK has already done this so you can apply to be a Coastguard pilot having never been in the military. You'll need a minimum of a CPL, type rating and IR. You'll often need a fair few flying hours too.

Firefighting Pilot

Salary Range $-$$
Role: As a firefighting pilot you'll operate aircraft equipped to combat wildfires by dropping water, fire retardant, or foam over affected areas. The role involves flying at low altitudes in challenging conditions to accurately release firefighting materials, often coordinating with ground crews and other aircraft.

You'll need excellent flying skills, precise control, and the ability to make quick decisions under pressure. This can be an extremely exciting role, however it definitely comes with its fair share of dangers and challenges. Operating any aircraft low level is dangerous, let alone over fires and usually undulating terrain that's inaccessible for ground vehicles.

Working Hours: Work hours can be irregular and demanding, especially during peak fire seasons, requiring availability for extended periods and rapid deployment. Expect time away from home and plenty of standby time.

Requirements: CPL and type rating on the aircraft operated. You'll also need to complete specialized training (usually provided by the employer)

Law Enforcement Pilot

Salary Range $$-$$$

Role: Fixed-wing law enforcement jobs are few and far between, but most countries do offer them. Infact, the UK Police are recruiting pilots for their fixed wing aircraft at the time of writing this. As well as aerial law enforcement units, areas in the US also operate anti-narcotics units to patrol coastlines.
You'll be doing almost exactly what police helicopter pilots do; you will fly on fast-paced, dynamic missions, working with Tactical Flight Officers to find missing people, follow dangerous vehicles, support firearms operations, gather criminal evidence and help police large-scale events. As you're in a fixed wing you'll have much greater range over police helicopters so you can assist callouts further afield. Due to the extended range, forces need fewer fixed wing aircraft based around the network which also means the jobs are harder to come by.

Working Hours: Generally, you'll be on a fixed roster pattern working shifts. It will involve working nights and weekends along with plenty of time on standby.

Requirements: Minimum of a CPL and IR. You'll also likely be required to have plenty of flight hours on top of the CPL.

Private Jet Pilot

Salary Range $$-$$$$$

Role: You'll operate private jets (otherwise known as business jets) on behalf of either wealthy individuals or large corporations. It's a role that once again will likely demand you wear multiple hats. Aswell as being the pilot, you'll often also be attending directly to your passengers' needs. Various tasks outside the scope of flying duties such as loading the passenger baggage can often be your role, as can in-flight service if you're on a smaller aircraft without a cabin crew member.

Larger companies will likely have their own flight planning department, but if you're operating for an individual owner, lots of these tasks will come down to you.

It's an interesting role that has a huge evariety of different types of jobs available within it. See our article in PilotBible's a 'A Day In The Life' section written by Tyler, a private jet pilot in the UAE to read a little more about the life.

Working Hours: If working for an individual who owns the jet, the hours are likely to be quite unpredictable with lots of time spent on standby, ready to prepare the jet whenever the owner needs it. Those who work for individuals tend to have high salaries.

If you're working for a larger private jet charter company (such as NetJets or VistaJet in the UK) then you're more likely to have a relatively stable roster, with fixed days on and off. Your working hours during your days on will likely entirely be decided by the requirements of your operations department.

Requirements: Minimum of a CPL & IR along with a type rating on that jet. Employers may also be looking for an ATPL too.

Airline Pilot

Salary Range $$-$$$$$

Role: You'll operate large commercial airliners carrying passengers domestically or internationally.

You'll usually start your airline career as a first officer in the right hand seat of a Jet whilst the captain occupies the left hand seat. Your primary role as a first officer will be to support the captain but also develop your own skills as you'll be in that seat one day.

The flying will be shared between both pilots, as will the management of communication and navigation. In a large airline, your flight plans will be pre-

prepared by a team and given to you on the day of the flight. You'll often do between 5-15 years as a first officer before undertaking a command course and becoming a captain.

First officer roles can often be low paid, however as you move up through the ranks at reputable airlines the pay can increase very rapidly. Currently in the US, airline captains are earning salaries of between $300k-$500k per year. This has inflated hugely in the last 2 years so it will be interesting to see if the salaries remain that high.

For more extensive information on the ins and out's of the airline industry, along with much more detail around this job role specifically and my recommendations of how best to get into this part of the industry, I've compiled all of this into its own book "How To Become An Airline Pilot" which you can find on amazon, on our website, or from any large aviation retailer in the UK or US. The airline world is *such* a large and varied one with its own complexities that there's enough to fill that book, whereas this book focusses more on giving you an overview of all the different options available to you and hopefully helping you decide which door you want to look further inside.

Working Hours: In the airline world you'll usually be on either a fixed or flexible roster. On a fixed roster you'll know exactly which days you'll be working a year from now. On a flexible roster, the airline decides your working days and you'll find these out when your roster gets published (usually around 1 month in advance). Airline work is mostly shift work and consists of long flying days, usually also working unsociable hours (& often weekends).

Your lifestyle will also greatly depend on whether you fly short haul or long haul;

Short Haul – You'll always operate from a 'home base'. You'll usually do

blocks of 5 – 6 days flying, then a few days off between. During those blocks on you'll likely be doing 2-4 flights each day. With some short haul carriers, you'll always end up back at home base every night. Others do 'tours' where each night you'll stopover in a different city.

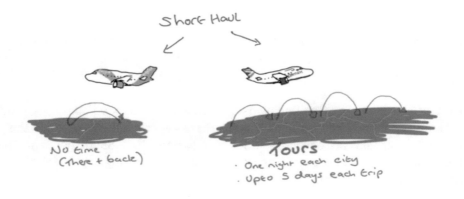

Short Haul

No time
(there + back)

Tours
· One night each city
· Upto 5 days each trip

Long Haul – You'll also be operating from a 'home base'. These however tend to be longer flights, and usually with a stopover the other end. Airlines have now caught onto the fact that paying their staff to lay on a beach down route isn't great for their profits, so long haul stopovers tend to be a lot shorter than they used to be. Whilst some legacy carriers do still give multiple night stopovers, it's not uncommon for crew to get just 24 hours from landing to departing again. Some airlines also operate 'bullets' whereby pilots operate a long-haul sector out, then fly straight back on the same aircraft as passengers. Long haul often means more time away from home than short haul. You'll also have jet lag to contend with!

Long Haul

24hrs → 5 days

Requirements: ATPL (Frozen ATPL usually acceptable) or MPL with a TR. Some airlines now cover the cost of your training if you're bonded to them. See our website or 'How To Become An Airline Pilot' book for more info.

Cargo Pilot

Salary Range $$-$$$$$

Role: As a cargo or freight pilot you'll be operating cargo aircraft, transporting goods and packages on scheduled or charter flights for logistics and shipping companies. These can be large global companies such as DHL or FedEx, or smaller independent companies. The flying side of things is reasonably similar to the role of an airline pilot (& you're flying very similar if not the same aircraft) however your crew will likely consist of just pilots, there are no cabin crew or passengers to deal with.

With the current pilot shortage some cargo pilots are earning more money than airline pilots.

Working Hours: The vast majority of your flights will be at night. Airports are generally much quieter at this time and slots are cheaper. Whilst it's tough operating through the night, the operation tends to always be much smoother and more on time than daytime flights partly due to the above reasons and partly as you don't have 200+ passengers to manage each flight!

Cargo pilots will usually be working predictable rosters and know their time off far in advance. They'll usually do 4 or 5 days of work followed by some days off. They can also sometimes do extended trips away from home.

Requirements: ATPL (Frozen is acceptable) or MPL with a TR.

Calibration Pilot

Salary Range $-$$$

Role: This is an extremely niche job but it's still worth mentioning. As a calibration pilot, you'll be flying a specially equipped aircraft into a huge variety of airports. Your job is to check the calibration on the 'instrument landing and approach' system the airport uses to guide aircraft into land. The job will consist of flying multiple approaches at each airport to check and re-calibrate the equipment before moving on to the next.

Working Hours: The company you fly for will likely have contracts in place with airports and set dates for calibration, therefore you're likely to have a relatively stable and predictable working roster.

Requirements: CPL, IR and TR.

Seaplane Pilot

Salary Range $-$$

Role: As a seaplane pilot you'll be operating an aircraft capable of taking off from and landing on water, whilst providing transportation services to remote locations, conducting scenic tours, or supporting various commercial and recreational activities.

You'll be trained how to master specialized techniques for water-based operations, including handling takeoffs, landings, and docking. Most of your flights will be into areas without traditional runways, such as lakes, rivers, and coastal regions. You'll need to develop a good understanding of the maritime world as well as the aviation world.

Working Hours: Similar to that of a sightseeing pilot

Requirements: CPL along with a specific rating to operate seaplanes

Experience Ride Pilot

Salary Range $-$$$

Role: In this role you'll provide exhilarating flying experiences for passengers, often including aerobatic manoeuvres such as loops, rolls, and spins.
The role involves ensuring the safety and comfort of passengers while delivering an exciting and memorable flight.
There are a variety of aircraft that companies operate for these experiences, from vintage WW2 aircraft all the way up to old military fighter jets.

Working Hours: Usually lots of weekend work as that's when people will tend to book in for their experience rides, although popular locations will also be busy throughout the week. The days may be long in Summer when the weather is good, but you'll almost always be sticking to daylight flying hours only. Hours may die off in the Winter.

Requirements: This will highly depend on the types of aircraft being operated. If it's older military aircraft, the preference would likely be ex-military personnel however there will usually be some scope for someone with a CPL to receive special training towards flying that type.

Rotary Pilot Roles

Do you like the thought of flying something that can hover, land almost anywhere and requires a high level of hand eye co-ordination to operate? Helicopters may be for you! Let's dive into the specific requirements for helicopter licences along with the different jobs available.

Licensing Requirements Helicopters	Privelidges	Hour Req	Written Exams	Medical Req	Estimated Total Cost
LAPL (EU)	Fly light aircraft up to certain weight	40 hrs flight training	9 x Written Exams	Class 3/LAPL	£23,000
PPL	Private flying with friends & family	45 hrs of flight training (EU)	9 x Written Exams	Class 2	£25,000
		40 hrs flight training (US)	1 x Written Exam	Class 3	$18,000
CPL	Get paid for flying	150 hrs flight time (EU)	14 x Written Exams	Class 1	£75,000 (incl PPL cost)
		150 hrs flight time (US)	1 x Written Exam	Class 2	$55,000 (inc PPL cost)
ATPL	Act in Command of large passenger aircraft	1000 hrs flight time (EU)	14 x Written Exams	Class 1	£100,000 +
		1200 hrs flight time (US)	1 x Written Exam		$100,000 +

To keep it simple again I've added only the basic hour requirements. For a more detailed table that breaks down the exact type of flight training hours required for each licence check out the PilotBible site or your aviation authority's website.

You'll notice the price of these licences are substantially more than their fixed wing counterparts. This is because helicopters are extremely expensive to purchase and maintain. They have even more rigorous maintenance and overhaul schedules than most fixed wing aircraft, and essentially have to be entirely re-built every certain number of years.

The training is also substantially less in the US than it is in the UK. It's quite common for people to go there from the UK or EU to build their flying hours, however you need to ensure the school you build your hours at will be approved by either the UK CAA or EASA, otherwise you may not get full credit for these hours when applying for a licence in Europe.

Sightseeing Helicopter Pilot

Salary Range $-$$

Role: Very similar to that of a fixed-wing sightseeing pilots, you'll be conducting aerial tours & providing passengers with scenic views from an aircraft. You'll be responsible for much of the same as in the fixed wing role. Helicopter sightseeing roles tend to be more varied as you have the ability to hover and also land off airport.

You could be operating tours over cities such as London or New York, whale watching in New Zealand, operating a helicopter safari in Africa, or flying through the Grand Canyon. Helicopters are often also used for mountain tours and even landing on glaciers. It all depends on which sort of company you want to join & what type of flying you want to be doing.

It can likely get repetitive if you're operating the same tour daily, however there are many tour and sightseeing providers out there so you have a lot of options available if you wanted to mix things up.

Many helicopter pilots use these roles to build their flying hours before moving onto other roles that have higher flight hour requirements to apply but often pay more money.

Working Hours: Highly dependent on the operation, although due to the nature of sightseeing its usually daytime working hours and weather dependant flying. Often much of your flying will be done at weekend, however in popular tourist locations you'll likely be flying in the week too.

Requirements: Minimum of a CPL(H) along with a type rating for the type of helicopter you'll be flying.

Helicopter Flight Instructor

Salary Range $-$$

Role: Providing ground and flight instruction for student pilots, covering fundamental aviation principles, flight manoeuvres and navigation. You'll also prepare students for various licensing exams. This position demands excellent flying skills, a deep understanding of aviation regulations, effective teaching abilities, and the capacity to adapt to different learning styles. You'll also likely be operating experience flights and trial lessons.

Being a helicopter instructor requires even sharper and more concentrated focus than fixed wing instructing as helicopters tend to be extremely sensitive to inputs and are more complex aircraft than their fixed-wing counterparts, requiring a higher level of coordination by the student to operate safely.

It can be an extremely rewarding career seeing your students progress and go on to get their own licence. Unfortunately helicopter instructing is also a notoriously low paid role.

Working Hours: The hours can be quite sporadic and very weather dependant. You'll often only get paid for the hours you actually fly, and smaller companies will only fly when a student books in.

Much of the work at smaller independent flight schools will be centred around weekends as most flight students will tend to work during the week to fund their training. If you join a larger flight school offering integrated courses as an instructor, the work will generally be more consistent as the students are full time.

Requirements: CPL(H) along with an FI rating. In addition an IR rating will make you more employable as an instructor but It's not always necessary.

Helicopter Charter Pilot

Salary Range $-$$$

Role: As a charter pilot you'll mainly be taking passengers from A to B safely and efficiently. You'll operate to a mix of on-airport and off-airport landing sites and will likely be operating into confined areas and private sites. Many of your passengers will be business professionals, tourists and VIPs (all probably with substantial sums of money!).

In smaller companies you'll be responsible for flight planning and managing many other tasks as well as just the flying. Larger companies will have teams to take care of these for you.

I know various pilots who do this role and love it. Often the flying varies day by day and it's a job where you do get some interaction with the passengers. Most charter helicopters will be single pilot (a very common charter helicopter is the A109) however some larger ones will require two pilots.

Salary in this role is totally dependent on the exact type of work you're doing. Most charter pilots working for a company are reasonably well paid and pilots tend to be there as a lifelong career, not just to gain flight hours.

Check out the piece in our 'Day In the life' section on our website by Raiyan, a helicopter charter pilot based in the UK for more info.

Working Hours: With larger companies you'll often have a fixed roster of days on & off. Charters are usually organised in advance so you'll also have some idea of your actual working hours, although the flights can always be changed closer to the time or even on the day.
Charter companies tend to be very busy during the Summer season as they often operate shuttle flights to/from major sporting events for those wanting to beat the traffic jams. This often means lots of weekend work and some very long days. Winter tends to be quieter however you'll have poor weather and more hours of darkness to contend with so it can still be challenging work.

Requirements: CPL(H) and type rating for the aircraft as minimum. In additional an IR rating will make you more employable but It's not always necessary. Companies operating large multi-crew helicopters such as an S92 may require you to have an ATPL(H).

Private Helicopter Pilot

Salary Range $$-$$$$

Role: This is similar to a charter pilot however you'll be flying for an individual owner. Because of this the flying can be extremely varied & you'll be operating the aircraft in whatever capacity the owner requires.

It could involve operating to/from landing decks on yachts. You could be operating sightseeing tours for the owner, or doing simple flights from A to B.

Most private helicopters will be single pilot however some larger ones will require two pilots (like James Dysons personal A139 picture above!). The salary can vary greatly depending on the individual you fly for, but you can often receive substantial sums of money in the form of a salary or tips.

Working Hours: If you're operating for an individual then quite often you will be required to go where they go and fly when they want to fly. Much of your time may be spent on standby and having to stay within proximity of the individual. Whilst this may work for some, the unpredictability and time away from home based on someone else's calander won't be ideal for others.

Requirements: CPL(H) & type rating for the aircraft. You'll also usually need a very high level of flight hours as owners with high net worth want to employ very safe and experienced pilots.

News/Media Helicopter Pilot

Salary Range $-$$

Role: You'll work for news stations providing aerial coverage of events, traffic conditions, and other stories for media outlets.

The role involves flying to various locations, often on short notice, to capture live footage and provide real-time updates from the air.

You'll be navigating airspaces and controlling the aircraft whilst also ensuring the helicopter is positioned optimally for the best camera angles. You'll have to be extremely situationally aware of other news and emergency service aircraft around you. During car chases in LA it's not uncommon to have multiple police helicopters along with multiple news helicopters all trying to follow the pursuit from above.

Working Hours: This job will involve shiftwork and weekend work. Whilst some of the flying may be predictable i.e daily traffic updates, much of your time at base will be spent waiting on standby, ready to start the engines as soon as you're requested to provide coverage.

Requirements: CPL(H) along with the relevant type rating

Offshore Helicopter Pilot

Salary Range $$-$$$

Role: You'll be transporting personnel and cargo between mainland and offshore installations such as oil rigs, wind farms, and research vessels. The role involves conducting flights over open water, often in challenging weather conditions, ensuring the safe and timely delivery of workers and essential supplies.

You'll usually do between 2 and 4 flying legs per day, sometimes between various rigs and then back to shore.

Offshore helicopter pilots perform detailed pre-flight planning, including weather assessment and fuel management, and execute precise and challenging landings onto confined platforms built onto oil rigs.

It's a role with lots of threats and challenges, and whilst flying you'll often have to wear a survival suit in case the helicopter ditches in the water. Check out the piece on our website by Maddy who operates the A139 to oil rigs in the North Sea to read more about a day in the life.

Working Hours: Larger operations will essentially run like airlines. They'll have proper rosters, and you'll know your flying days well in advance. Big companies in the UK such as Bristow have various part time options for pilots too.

The hours will be shift work but they're often more stable and predictable than fixed-wing airlines. The flying will be weather dependant too, however you'll still be expected to fly in some extremely tough weather conditions and also at night. You'll likely work across weekends too.

Requirements: Usually a CPL(H), type rating for the aircraft along with an IR as a minimum. Some companies may require an ATPL (H).

Utility Pilot

Salary Range $-$$

Role: This could be power line inspection, pipeline patrol or aerial survey & mapping. You'll fly specially equipped helicopters, often in very close proximity to the ground and power lines. You'll usually be using a thermal imaging camera to check the condition of the power lines, gas pipes & various structures, occasionally carrying out repairs on them too.

You'll have an observer onboard whose job it is to carry out inspections, whilst your primary role will be to safely control the aircraft. Most of your working days are spent travelling at very low speed in straight lines, and you'll always be operating at low level and extremely close to wires & other potentially lethal hazards so it's an extremely engaging job requiring constant focus.

Working Hours: Usually a very stable roster pattern. Due to the hazards involved its often daylight flying hours only. Most companies will have 2 shifts per day i.e early and late. Whilst the schedule may change if emergency repairs or inspections are required, most of the flying will be planned far ahead of time.

Requirements: Usually a CPL(H), and a type rating for the aircraft. Companies also tend to favour employing helicopter pilots who are either ex-military, or have experience operating Police or medical helicopters due to the low level experience that comes with these roles.

Military Helicopter Pilot

Salary Range $-$$$

Role: You'll operate state of the art military helicopters to support a wide range of missions, including combat operations, troop transport, reconnaissance, and medical evacuations.

Your exact tasks will depend on which type of helicopter you get streamed onto after your basic flight training. Military helicopters are typically divided into different categories. You've got attack helicopters such as Apache's. You've also got logistics and transport helicopter such as the Chinook. Different forces will operate different helicopters, but you'll conduct missions together i.e in the UK, the Army fly the Apache and the RAF fly the Chinook, but the two will work together on missions.

You'll likely be flying in diverse and hostile environments, executing precise manoeuvres, and coordinating closely with ground and air units to achieve mission objectives.

This position demands exceptional flying skills, strategic thinking, and the ability to perform under extreme pressure, all while maintaining the highest standards of safety and mission effectiveness. The flying will possibly be the most exhilarating yet challenging that you can legally do in a helicopter, with plenty of low level sorties, close formation and night flying.

Working Hours: Training tends to be mostly Mon-Fri hours. Once qualified, you'll be sent away on 'tours' for several months at a time.
On some tours there will be routine flights conducted at the same time each day i.e patrols, whilst other flying missions will be more unpredictable. Missions whilst on tour will likely involve plenty of night flying.

Requirements: Join the military, passing their selection process & basic training, followed by basic flight training before being streamed onto helicopters. You'll then undergo rigorous training to master advanced aviation techniques, combat tactics, and the operation of specialized equipment and weaponry.

Helicopter Medical Pilot

Salary Range $$-$$$

Role: There are many different terms for this role depending on where you are in the world – HEMS (Helicopter Emergency Medical Service, Heli-Med, Medevac (Medical Evacuation), EMS (Emergency Medical Service) and they are all essentially the same job.

Your primary task will be delivering specialist medical personal and their equipment directly to the scene of an incident. You'll also be flying critically ill or injured patients from the scene to medical facilities, and operating hospital transfers for other patients who are too poorly to be transferred by land ambulance.

It's a fast paced role that brings with it plenty of challenges but also huge rewards. You're on the front line saving lives and every minute counts.

Due to the nature of accidents and emergencies, you often don't have much time to plan your flights. In the daytime you'll often be starting your engines as soon as you hear a call come in. You'll be given priority over other air traffic as you make your way to scene, and once on-scene be expected to land the helicopter as close as you safely can to the casualty. This can mean landing on roads, beaches, in parks and on playgrounds.

It's one of the only helicopter jobs out there that brings this type of variety, and also the ability to land a helicopter in urban areas on a daily basis.

You'll work closely with your medical team onboard and be liaising with other emergency services on the ground. You'll often need to get roads closed by the police ahead of your arrival if you're planning to land on the road.

It's often a high-stress job and you'll also see some things that may be unpleasant as you're often only dispatched to the most traumatic incidents, but it's one of few pilot jobs where you can directly see the impact you're having on people's lives.

Some units run single pilot operations, so it will be yourself and two or three medical personnel on the aircraft, whereas larger aircraft such as the AW169 which is becoming a highly popular HEMS aircraft will require 2 flight crew. You'll usually be stationed at a base which is where you'll start and end all of your flying, however companies also employ 'touring' pilots whereby you can be sent to various bases to operate their helicopters.

Check out the "Day In The Life Of" piece on our site by Samantha who's an EMS pilot in the Rocky Mountains for more info on this.

Working Hours: Usually a very stable roster pattern, albeit with challenging work hours. You'll often work a few days on followed by a few days off. Your working days will likely be long (up to 12 hour shifts) with pretty much all of it spent on standby ready for the dispatch phone to ring with a job location.

Some HEMS operations are daylight hours only, however with technological advances such as night vision goggles (NVGs) and enhanced software mapping of hazards such as wires and other obstacles, many operators now also work through the night. Selfishly people still have accidents on weekends so expect to be working then too.

Requirements: CPL(H) & type rating for the aircraft, usually along with an IR. Some companies may require an ATPL (H). Companies also tend to favour pilots who are either ex-military, however there are plenty of pilots now moving into the HEMS space from civilian flying.

Coastguard / Search and Rescue Pilot

Salary Range $$-$$$

Role: I've joined these two roles together as there's huge amounts of crossover between them. They're also sometimes operated by the same crew & aircraft. In both roles you'll be conducting aerial missions to locate and rescue individuals in distress, often in challenging maritime and coastal environments.

The role involves flying in various weather conditions to perform search patterns, hoist operations, and medical evacuations. You'll work closely with ground based rescue teams and sometimes other airborne teams to coordinate efforts and ensure the safe extraction of people from dangerous situations and incidents.

Search and Rescue (SAR) crews will often be operating in mountainous areas and in poor weather conditions which brings with it a multitude of threats.

This position demands exceptional flying skills, proficiency in specialized rescue techniques, and the ability to make quick, critical decisions under pressure. Most Coastguard and SAR aircraft are now multi-crew operations so you'll have two pilots in the flightdeck along with winchmen, paramedics and observers in the rear of the aircraft.

Working Hours: You'll usually work multiple days at a time on standby, available to be called out anytime of the day. This will then be followed by a block of days off. Rosters are usually fixed and built in advance so you know when your days off will be, however your actual hours flown on your days on will be dictated by the incidents you need to respond to.

Requirements: CPL(H) & type rating for the aircraft, usually along with an IR. Some companies may require an ATPL (H). Both Coastguard and SAR were traditionally government or military owned and would therefore only use military pilots, however many of these services are becoming privatised and employing pilots with no armed force experience. You'll likely need a lot of rotary flying hours before being considered, and will have to undergo a lot of specialist training before starting the job.

For more insights, check out the article in our 'Day in the life of' section on our website written by Gav, a helicopter recuse pilot in Australia.

Law Enforcement Helicopter Pilot

Salary Range $-$$$

Role: As a law enforcement helicopter pilot, you'll support operations by providing aerial surveillance, rapid response, and logistical support to ground based law enforcement during various missions.

Your role will include patrolling urban and rural areas, assisting in search and pursuit of suspects, monitoring large public events, and coordinating with ground units to enhance situational awareness and operational effectiveness.

The role can be highly varied depending on where in the world you operate. If you fly for the LAPD (Los Angeles Police Department), you'll fly for the majority of the day. If there are no response calls, you'll spend your time doing low level beach and city patrols. In the UK, NPAS (National Police Air Support Unit) tend to remain on the ground on standby unless an emergency call comes in or you're tasked to oversee certain events. Often for football games and other large sporting events, especially in London or other big cities, they will have a police helicopter sending live visual feeds to a control room so police coordinators on the ground can monitor what's going on. You'll often have 2 helicopter units rotating being airborne so there's always one 'eye in the sky' when one helicopter needs to return to base to refuel.

Either way you'll be operating a highly equipped aircraft with a very well-trained group of people. Usually 1-2 flight crew, with at least one observer/tactical flight officer who will also be a trained police officer.

Working Hours: The shifts will be very similar to that of the medical helicopter pilots, so usually a very stable and fixed roster pattern for days on and off. It's still shift work so expect to be operating in both day and night, also across weekends.

Requirements: CPL(H) & type rating for the aircraft, usually along with an IR. Some forces may require an ATPL (H). Some units will require pilots to have previously served time as a police officer, others do not.

Firefighting Helicopter Pilot

Salary Range $-$$

Role: As a firefighting helicopter pilot you'll operate helicopters equipped to combat wildfires by dropping water or fire retardant and transporting firefighting crews and equipment to fire zones.
Your role will involve flying at low altitudes in challenging conditions to accurately release firefighting materials and assist ground crews in controlling and extinguishing fires.
You'll be refilling either the aircrafts water tanks directly, or an external bucket, from a water source near the fire. This can be lakes, the ocean, or even peoples private swimming pools! Obviously operating helicopters near fires and water at low level, with underslung load brings with it inherent risks.

Working Hours: Very similar to fixed wing firefighting, the hours can be irregular and demanding, especially during peak fire seasons, requiring availability for extended periods and rapid deployment. Expect time away from home and plenty of time spent on standby.

Requirements: CPL(H) & type rating for the aircraft. You'll also need to undertake specialist firefighter training usually organised and sponsored by the employer.

Humanitarian Helicopter Pilot

Salary Range $-$$

Role: You'll provide critical air transport services for humanitarian missions, often in regions affected by conflict, natural disasters, or inaccessible terrain.

You'll deliver essential supplies such as food, medicine, and relief personnel to remote or crisis-stricken areas.

Whilst the government do often provide much of the above using military aircraft and personnel, the work can be contracted out to other organizations. A prime example of this is Columbia Helicopters, a company which carries out a wide variety of work in their chinook helicopters including humanitarian work.

The lovely Charlie who flies for Columbia kindly answered all our questions on what life is like on humanitarian missions and that article can be found on our 'Day In The Life' blog area on our website.

Working Hours: Given the nature of the role, you'll find yourself away from home a lot. Whilst on a mission (which could be anything from a few days to a few months) you'll likely be based near the area you're operating in and working long days. Once home you'll often get substantial periods of time off.

Requirements: CPL(H) & type rating for the aircraft. Some companies may also require you to have an ATPL if operating larger more complexed multi-crew aircraft.

Agricultural Helicopter Pilot

Salary Range $-$$

Role: Similarly to fixed wing, you'll be operating aircraft to apply fertilizers, pesticides, herbicides, and seeds over agricultural fields. Your time will be spent flying at low altitudes navigating obstacles such as power lines and trees. With a helicopter you'll be landing on top of a rig or truck to refill the spraying tanks too.

Low hour CPL holders will usually do crop-dusting to build hours whilst also gaining the experience of flying an aircraft at very low level.

Working Hours: Daytime hours, usually a stable and predictable working life.

Requirements: CPL(H) & type rating for the aircraft.

Filming/Stunt Helicopter Pilot

Salary Range $-$$

Role: For anyone who's already enthusiastic about the helicopter industry, I'm sure you've heard of Fred North. If you haven't then go check out his social media channels. He's a helicopter filming pilot and also a stunt pilot. Whilst his role is admittedly a rare one (& becoming even rarer due to the advancements in drones capable of high quality filming) there are still various similar roles out there.

The role will involve lots of low level and hands-on flying. It will require extremely accurate flying skills in order to get the correct filming shots, along with performing stunts if needs be.

Working Hours: Quite an unpredictable schedule. Totally dependent on the requirements of the film crew. Mix of day & nighttime hours. Often time away from home whilst on set.

Requirements: CPL(H) & type rating for the aircraft. You'll also need experience flying low level and in challenging flying conditions. Most employers will require a high number of flying hours and many of these jobs will be word of mouth rather than advertised online.

Aerial lift Helicopter Pilot

Salary Range $-$$

Role: Large helicopters have the ability to lift and manoeuvre underslung loads (objects attached to the bottom of the helicopter using long lines). Many different industries have taken advantage of this and helicopters now form an essential part of their daily work.

There are many different aerial lift operations out there, from aerial crane work (this can be on construction sites, or moving items from a-b that are inconvenient to move in any other manner) to logging (supporting logging operations by transporting logs from remote or inaccessible areas to processing facilities or onto the back of lorries for further transport by road). Aerial lifting is notoriously challenging due to the precise nature of flying required along with the dangers of having large swinging loads attached to your helicopter.

Working Hours: Likely daytime only and often Mon-Fri, however this isn't a hard and fast rule.

Requirements: CPL(H) & type rating for the aircraft. Will also need specialist training in the type of lifting you wish to do.

Wildlife Conservation Helicopter Pilot

Salary Range $-$$

Role: You'll support wildlife conservation by conducting aerial surveys, monitoring wildlife populations, and assisting in conservation research and management activities.

The role involves flying over diverse terrains and ecosystems to track animal movements, identify habitats, and document environmental changes.

You'll work closely with biologists, researchers, and conservationists, providing crucial aerial support for projects such as animal relocation, habitat restoration, and anti-poaching patrols.

The job will involve lots of low-level hands-on flying, occasionally having to get close enough to animals for vets to be able to shoot tranquilizing darts out the side of the aircraft into the animal if it's in need of medical care.

Working Hours: Likely daytime only. It may mean time away from home whilst you do this job as they're usually based deep within the bush in places like Africa.

Requirements: CPL(H) & type rating for the aircraft.

Other Pilot Roles

As well as the standard fixed-wing and rotary categories, there are some flying roles that fall into more niche ones.

Balloon Pilot

Salary Range $-$$

Role: You'll operate hot air balloons or airships, providing passengers with scenic and recreational flights.

Your role will include checking weather conditions, selecting launch and landing sites, and preparing the balloon for flight. During the flight, you'll manage the burner system to control altitude and navigate by using wind currents at different altitudes. Part of your job will also be to provide an enjoyable customer experience. Balloon pilots can't choose a specific landing site before they takeoff so whilst you're airborne, your ground crew will be following you in vehicles and will meet you wherever you do end up landing to help deflate and pack away the balloon.

Working Hours: You'll usually be working early in the morning or during the evening as this is often when conditions are best for balloons. Work will be very weather dependant and if you live in a country with unpredictable weather you can expect to regularly be having to cancel and re-schedule flights. Work is usually only in the summer months and you're unlikely to do more than 2 balloon flights per day.

Requirements: Balloon Pilots Licence (BPL) and clearance to fly the class of balloon you're operating. In the UK you'll need a Class 2 medical certificate.

Sailplane Pilot

Salary Range $

Role: Otherwise known as gliders, operating a sailplane will entail skilfully using natural air currents to stay aloft and navigate. You'll launch the glider using a winch or tow aircraft, then find and exploit thermal updrafts, ridge lifts, and other atmospheric phenomena to maintain flight. Sailplane pilots focus on efficient energy management, precise control, and keen observation of weather patterns. You'll can engage in competitive gliding, cross-country flights, and recreational soaring.

Gliding is often only done for recreational purposes and rarely as a job. The only job role tends to be conducting experience flights and instructing student sailplane pilots.

Working Hours: Daytime hours and fair weather only. Often flying will be focussed on weekends.

Requirements: Sailplane Pilots Licence (SPL) or Light Aircraft Pilots Licence (LAPL). In the UK you'll need a Class 2 medical certificate.

Drone Pilot

Salary Range $-$$

Role: Whilst I'm sure there are some pilots out there who will dispute this role being in this book, operators of drones are still classed as pilots, so I believe it has a place here.

The size and purpose of drones varies greatly, as do the job roles available. The military operate extremely large unmanned aerial vehicles (UAVs) into conflict zones for surveillance and attack missions. The drone pilot can often be controlling the drone from the other side of the world.

Other drone roles include commercial purposes such as photography and filming work, along with surveys. The UK police now have drones that fly with thermal imaging cameras to help them locate criminals near the scene of crimes.

Working Hours: Completely dependent on the purpose of use. Military and police drone pilots will be working shift work. Commercial drone pilots will often be working daytime hours only.

Requirements: In the UK if you wish to operate a drone with a weight over 250g you must apply to do so with the CAA.

EVTOL Pilot

Salary Range N/A

Role: This is more a potential job of the future. During my time working for an aviation tech start-up I began to see a new pattern emerging in the aviation industry. Companies are racing to build electric flying vehicles capable of vertical takeoff and landing known as eVTOL's.

The use case will be urban air mobility missions, such as passenger transport, cargo delivery, and emergency services, often in densely populated areas. These aircraft merge the capabilities of helicopters and fixed wing aircraft in a more efficient and sustainable way than has previously been attempted.

Whilst many of these aircraft are still in the testing phase, the companies creating them have received huge levels of funding from major players in the industry such as Boeing (one company got a £250M investment from Boeing) and Lockheed Martin. Examples of eVTOL companies are Volocopter, Joby and Vertical.

Some companies are planning to build completely autonomous eVTOLs however many companies are designing aircraft that require pilots. I strongly believe this is an industry that will see huge growth over the next decade and require thousands of pilots to be trained to safely operate these machines.

Working Hours: Currently unknown but likely to be shift work, operating set routes daily.

Requirements: Unknown.

Next Steps

So you've now read the book and absorbed lots of the information. What's next for you? My recommendation would be the following;

Trial lesson

If you haven't actually had a go at getting behind the controls of an aircraft yet, that's a very important first step to take. It's not so much to see if you're any good at it, it's more to see if you actually enjoy it!

Get yourself a trial lesson in the category of aircraft (fixed wing or rotary) that you think you'd be most interested in flying. Trial lessons usually last between 30 minutes and an hour and are usually very fairly priced. It's a great introduction to flying and you'll be able to have a go at flying the aircraft with an instructor next to you. If you can't afford one of these maybe ask your family if they could gift it to you for a birthday or Christmas present?

Research

So you've now flown an actual aircraft and you're pretty sure you want to do this more! The next step is to do more thorough research into the exact roles you'd be interested in, along with the medical, educational and flying requirements to get that role. Follow the guidance at the start of the book for the best research methods.

Once you've got your heart set on a certain role, or maybe like the sound of a few, you'll then need to research flight schools to find the one that best works for you. If you're looking to gain a CPL or higher, I'd recommend really taking your time in finding a flight school that's right for you. Go down and meet the staff, take a look at their aircraft and operation and try to get a feel whether it's a place you'd like to invest a substantial amount of your time and money with. Also ensure you read reviews online and ideally speak to current or past students of the school about their experience.

Finally, you'll have to research the financial side of things. The higher the level of licence you're going for, the more research and planning will have to go into this. Some schools offer sponsorships, and airlines offer fully funded courses, so time spent researching these options here can save you copious amounts in the long run. Take a look at the companies mentioned earlier in the book along with the recommended resources in the back.

Once you've decided on what sort of role you want, along with the best training path to get the right licence for you, the next step is to pull the trigger and enrol in a course!

Thanks for reading. I really hope you've been able to extract value from the book & best of luck on your pilot journey!

If you have any more questions, please feel free to message me at team@pilotbible.com or contact through our socials.

Captain Sam

Recommended Resources

Below are the main companies and resources I'd recommend to help you on your journey

One of the best forum sites out there. Huge selection of current, past, and wannabe pilots using it. There's a thread for almost anything. The wannabe forum will be helpful for anyone starting out.

Our handy blog site. Aimed to give you insights into the day of the life in various different pilot roles around the world. You can also read the 'Diary of an Airline Captain' to see what the day to day really consists of!

Great resource to keep up to date with the flight training world. Check here for the lates sponsorships available.

One of the most up-to date and comprehensive aviation information websites out there. The founders do a superb job of breaking down complex aviation topics into easily digestible and understandable articles, with extremely high-quality explanations. A site you'll definitely want to add to your bookmarks!

Pilot Selection and Training

The best and most up to date aptitude training platform out there for airline pilots. They've kindly offered a **10-euro discount** to anyone who's purchased this book. Follow the relevant link on this page to activate your discount.

 Another good source of CV and general career help. Sign up for lots of free information that can help you through the process.

 One of the UKs leading sites for everything aviation. They help you with everything, from ATPL flashcards, right through to booking simulators and revalidating licenses. They've got great question banks on there too!

 Sporty's Pilot Shop is the world's largest pilot shop, training and equipping pilots since 1961! With same day shipping & returns, Pilot tested & approved products, a best price promise and great guarantees, it's a superb resource for pilots globally.

Pilot General

 UK aircrew's go-to place when looking for accommodation. It's a great platform for anyone looking for a room near their base. They have long & short-term accommodation available at all major UK bases. Use code **CREW for 3 days free premium access.**

 A leading site for searching and securing for current and upcoming vacancies in the aviation sector

 The best pilot sunglasses (in my personal opinion!). They're the only ones that I can comfortable wear all day long including with my headset on. Follow this link for 10% off.

 The leading digital logbook company. They're offering **12-23% off** for our readers on their digital logbook products! See PilotBible's 'Pilot Essentials' page to apply the discount.

 Flightstore have been kitting out pilots and aircraft enthusiasts ever since we started back in 1999. With unrivalled levels of service and a huge range of stocked products, they're a great shop for any of your aviation needs.

 Pooleys have set the industry standard in so many areas of manufacturing and publishing of aviation products that other companies, over the years, have strived to emulate. Their 3000 products are now sold to over 100 countries around the world.

Airplan Flight Equipment is Europe's principle publisher and distributor of pilot supplies and flying training products. AFE's customers include leading flying schools and gliding clubs, major airlines, the armed forces, aircraft manufacturers, leading maintenance companies and tens of thousands of individual aircraft owners and pilots worldwide. They aim to offer the best service and most competitive prices across the widest stock range and I can testify that they achieve it!

The Air League is a UK based charity aiming to support the next generation of aviation by offering various programmes and flying scholarships, with over 100 scholarships given in 2023 alone. It's well worth a look for anyone wanting to get into aviation.

Founded in 2016, Aileron offers professional and aspiring pilots a unique way to log and preserve flight hours through beautifully crafted, personalized leather logbooks and digital solutions. Transform your flight records into a timeless keepsake.

Enjoy a **15% discount** with code **PILOT15** for PilotBible readers

---

☆ Did You Enjoy This Book? ☆

If you enjoyed the book, I'd be super grateful if you could spare 30 seconds to leave it an Amazon review. Simply scan the QR code and share your thoughts to help the book reach others like you!

Scan To Review

Other titles available from the author:

If you've completed this book and decided you want to become an airline pilot, this title is for you. It's an in-depth guide that will walk you through all the specifics of entering the airline world. It'll help you pass the selection process and give you the best chance possible of landing the airline job you want. Available in e-book & paperback on Amazon and with all main aviation retailers.

Scan To View

Made in United States
Troutdale, OR
12/19/2024

26782238R00055